Hong Kong Volunteers in Battle

A Record of the Actions of the
Hongkong Volunteer
Defence Corps
in the
Battle for Hong Kong
December 1941

Evan Stewart

First Published 1953
Reprinted 1956
by
YE OLDE PRINTERIE, LTD
Hong Kong

Reprinted 1970, 1982, 1989 and 1991
by
PRINTRITE
Hong Kong

Republished 2004
by
RHKR (The Volunteers) Association Ltd
www.rhkr.org
and in 2005 and 2007
by
Blacksmith Books
Hong Kong

Republished 2011 and 2020 for
The Royal Hong Kong Regiment (The Volunteers) Association
by
Blacksmith Books
Unit 26, 19/F, Block B, Wah Lok Industrial Estate
37-41 Shan Mei Street, Fo Tan, Hong Kong
www.blacksmithbooks.com

ISBN 978-988-79638-4-4

The General Officer Commanding British
Troops in China in December 1941,
Major-General C. M. Maltby M.C,
closed his dispatch of 21st November 1945
on the Operations in Hong Kong
from 8th to 25th December 1941
with the a tribute to the
Hong Kong Volunteer Defence Force

"In closing my dispatch I wish to pay a special tribute to the Hong Kong Volunteer Defence Corps. They proved themselves to be a valuable portion of the garrison. In peace they had surrendered a great deal of their leisure to training, their mobilization was completed smoothly and quickly, and in action they proved themselves stubborn and gallant soldiers. To quote examples seems almost invidious but I should like to place on record the superb gallantry of No. 3 (Eurasian) Company at Wong Nei Chong Gap and of No. 1 Battery who undertook infantry defence in the Stanley area, while the efficiency and gallantry of their Signal section and dispatch riders were outstanding".

Major-General C. M. Maltby's dispatch was submitted to the Secretary of State for War on 21 November 1945 and published in the London Gazette on 29 January 1948.

CONTENTS

Introduction

In Memory of the Members of the
Hong Kong Defence Corps

We enlisted in the Hong Kong Volunteer Defence Corps as a sense of duty, knowing very little of what the future held for us. As the battle continued, some were more fortunate than others in the dangers that we faced.

Those who survived the battle then had three years and eight months in captivity in Hong Kong or, for some of us, in Japan.

After the surrender, I spent some time with my family in Sydney, before eventually returning to Hong Kong. Today, I still remember the many of my comrades who were less fortunate.

Hong Kong Volunteers in Battle is in memory of them.

2838 Pte Robert Lapsley of No 2 Company HKVDC

May 2020

Sydney, Australia

Foreword to the 2020 Edition

When "A Record of the Actions of the Hong Kong Volunteer Defence Corps in the Battle for Hong Kong" was first published in 1953, the author was keen that the actions should be properly recorded for the benefit of future generations. These actions were recorded within the context of the overall battle fought by British Forces of which the HKVDC formed a part and this record was never intended to be a record of the whole battle. Actions by the non-HKVDC units were only recorded in so far as they were relevant to the overall battle and that of the HKVDC. The author would never have realised that in 2020, almost 70 years later, there would still be an interest in the Record.

As life in Hong Kong returned to normal after the Japanese occupation, volunteer soldiering was re-established in 1949 as the Hong Kong Defence Force, with Naval, Army and Air-Force units, gaining the title change to "Royal" on 1 May 1951. Conscription ended in 1961 and, in the same year, the Regiment was granted the title of "The Volunteers".

In 1970 the Naval unit was phased out with the army and air-force units continuing as The Royal Hong Kong Regiment (The Volunteers) and the Royal Hong Kong Auxiliary Air-Force. The Regiment disbanded in September 1995 with the The Royal Hong Kong Regiment (The Volunteers) Association continuing to provide the links between previous Volunteers and taking on many of the responsibilities of the Regiment. These include the republication of the Record of the Defence Corps' Actions under the shortened title of "Hong Kong Volunteers in Battle".

This book is significant in that it was written by those who took part in the actions described, and authored by one who was injured and continued to fight with distinction. Hence in republication the text remains unchanged as, to change it, could be regarded as a rewrite of history. However corrections have been made to mis-spelt names and military ranks based on more recent and more extensive record searches than were available to to the author; foot notes identify the changes made.

In this edition the two maps in the book have been replaced by seven new maps to show details of the Japanese Advance and to note the location of all places named in the book. These places would have been familiar to readers in 1953, but many have since disappeared while others are now seldom known by their old names. Names of towns and villages are given as spelt in the Record and not necessarily as now spelt.

An index of British Forces units and those named in the Report is now also included. As the Record is of the HKVDC's actions, this index extends to platoon level of the HKVDC units; it is thus hoped that this will facilitate research on individual HKVDC members and the sub units in which they served.

The book, under its original title, did not include the name of the author, Evan Stewart. The reasons were a mixture of modesty and impatience on the part of the author. The book was started in the prisoners of war camp when commanders were brought together under the leadership of Major Evan Stewart to record their knowledge of the events. As a result the extremely modest Major Evan Stewart was reluctant to put his name to the book as he thought it should be in the name of all the Volunteers who fought and died. However, it was decided that there would be a Foreword, written by someone relevant and distinguished, which would identify the author.

In the event several people said that they would be delighted to write this foreword, but all felt that the honour should be with others. With a deadline to meet, Major Evan Stewart pushed ahead with publication on the assumption that further editions would include his name as the author. This was not to be until the book was republished by the Regimental Association in 2004 in conjunction with the 150th Anniversary of the Founding of the Corps of Volunteers.

In accordance with Evan Stewart's desire that the book should be in the name of all the Volunteers who fought and died, the nominal roll of all of those who were on strength of the Hong Kong Volunteer Defence Corps on 9 December 1941 were added. With subsequent republications a list of those who received awards for their actions either in the battle or subsequently were added together with a brief history of Major Evan Stewart who died in 1958 at the age of 66 mainly from the effects of being a prisoner-of-war. At that time he was still Headmaster of St Paul's College and Honorary Colonel of the Hong Kong Regiment.

Evan Stewart was one of the unfortunate group whose lives were shortened by the lack of proper medical treatment while a Prisoner-of-War. Post war he joined the newly created Hong Kong Volunteer Defence Force, commanded the Home Guard Squadron and later was appointed Honorary Colonel to the Regiment, a position which he still held when he died in 1958. In June 1953 he led the contingent from the then current Volunteer unit, the Royal Hong Kong Defence Force, to take part in the parade which formed part of the coronation of Queen Elizabeth II, the sovereign of Great Britain and the head of the British Commonwealth.

3

His report of the visit was published in the 1953 Volunteer Magazine and is reproduced in Appendix VII as a tribute to him and for the benefit of the many readers who will never have witnessed such pomp and ceremony of a British coronation. This is supplemented by Appendix VIII which includes two tributes to Evan Stewart, the first by Brigadier Lindsay Ride who, in 1942, formed and led the British Army Aid Group in China while the Japanese occupied Hong Kong. He was later appointed Commandant of the Hong Kong Defence Force on its formation in 1949. The second is by Major Bevan Field, who served under Evan in No 3 Company and later was second in command of the Regiment.

The details included in the appendices would not have been possible without reference to both published and unpublished records and the help provided by individuals. The assistance provided is duly acknowledged with thanks and publications from which details have been obtained are:

- Not the Slightest Chance by Tony Banham – Hong Kong University Press
- British Army Aid Group by Edwin Ride – Oxford
- Colonial Office Circular Hong Kong – Official List of Civilian Internees – Held in the HK University Library Special Collections
- Commonwealth War Graves Commission on-line records
- The London Gazette on-line records

Individuals who have assisted include:

- Colonel Michael Stewart OBE, TD, DL on details of his father
- Tony Banham on the fate of so many after the surrender
- Elizabeth Ride on names of those who went on to serve in the BAAG and Force 136
- Solomon Bard, Henry Ching and James Hayes on those who received honours and awards
- Philip Cracknell on the location of many places whose names have changed since the time of the Battle
- Andy C. Neilson of King & Country for the design of the cover to this and previous editions

Particular thanks to Robert Lapsley of No 2 Company HKVDC who now lives in Sydney, Australia for his introduction to the Book.

Ronald Taylor

Hong Kong

July 2020

Foreword

(As included in the 1953 edition of A Record of the Action of the Hong Kong Volunteer Defence Corps in the Battle for Hong Kong December 1941)

In justice to the officers and men of the garrison of Hong Kong, it will be well to place on record certain points which, though obvious to us at the time, may not be equally obvious to future historians.

The requirements of empire strategy in other theatres of war rendered it impossible for full provision to be made for troops forming the garrison, who were consequently deficient of much essential material. We were lamentably weak as regards sea and air power; we had few anti-aircraft batteries, and those we had were very short of ammunition for training purposes; we had no radio-location equipment; the infantry battalions were, until just before the actual outbreak of war, without mortars, weapons on which the enemy so largely relied; and, owing to shortage of manpower we had to rely for transport mainly on personnel whose reliability was very much an unknown quantity.

It was especially unfortunate that the situation in other theatres of war had not permitted earlier despatch of infantry mortars and ammunition. Ammunition for the three-inch mortars arrived in November 1941, and then only 70 rounds per battalion - for practice and war. The men had had no previous practice or preliminary shooting with the two-inch mortar; in fact, two-inch ammunition was actually served out in battle. There was neither pack-mule equipment nor carrying equipment for the three-inch mortars.

Our inability to make air reconnaissance was a serious handicap; our only knowledge of enemy dispositions and troop movements was obtained from ground observation, and was limited to such enemy forces as were actually in contact with our troops. The impossibility of making sea reconnaissance, and our consequent uncertainty regarding the safety of the south coast of the island, necessitated our keeping troops in places where enemy landings might be made. This reduced the number of troops available as reserves for counter-attacks. Our scanty forces had to guard the whole coast-line of the island as well as cope with an invading force at one particular point.

The Japanese domination of the air not only enabled them to observe our positions and troop movements and direct their artillery fire, but also to use their air-force to cover infantry attacks. In the later stages of the fighting, their dive-bombing attacks played an important part in their capture of Mount Cameron and advance along the line of the gaps. Furthermore, the scanty opposition to the frequent enemy air-raids had a disheartening effect, on our troops, particularly during the last few days when the enemy aircraft were able to attack us almost with impunity.

In addition to the advantages which the Japanese possessed in complete sea and air domination, and their enormous preponderance in artillery, they had considerable superiority in numbers of fighting-men. They put into the field three divisions against our two brigades. In addition, during the fighting on the island, our troops, for reasons given above, had to maintain static defence, and it was thus possible for the Japanese to throw overwhelming numbers against one particular sector.

Japanese agents had an easy time during the period immediately preceding the outbreak of hostilities. Until the actual declaration of war it was impossible for us to take action against Japanese nationals and pro-Japanese Chinese in the Colony. The enemy had complete maps of the island, on which our fixed positions were shown. On both mainland and island Japanese troops were led by local guides, sometimes willingly, more often under compulsion. Saboteurs disrupted our communications and, in one instance, actually cut the "leads" of a demolition after the covering-party had withdrawn. Armed enemy agents sniped our troops at night; others were caught signalling to the Japanese troops. We learned later that several local Japanese, some of them well-known, had received citations for the work they had done prior to and during the period of hostilities.

The Defence Plan

Previous to November 1941, when the garrison comprised four regular battalions, the Defence Plan had been that one infantry battalion, the 2/14 Punjab Regiment, should operate on the mainland, fighting delaying actions. This battalion was to make its final withdrawal to Devil's Peak Peninsula, where the Ma Lau Tong Line had been constructed. Two infantry battalions, the 2nd Royal Scots and the 5/7 Rajputs, and one machine-gun battalion, the 1st Middlesex, together with the HKVDC were to form the island defence. Two HKVDC units, the Field Company Engineers and the Mobile Machine Gun Company, were also to operate on the mainland; the Field Company being responsible for the road and railway demolitions and the MMG as covering troops.

On the news of the despatch of the two Canadian battalions, a new Defence Plan was prepared. This was modelled on a plan suggested in 1938. It was decided to have a complete brigade on the mainland, and to hold the enemy there as long as possible. Detailed reconnaissance work was carried out, and the so-called "Gin-Drinkers Line" was selected. Work on this was pushed forward rapidly despite the fact that it was the malarial season. The Royal Scots, who were working in the vicinity of Tsun Wan, a notoriously unhealthy district, suffered severely.

The new plan also entailed an alteration in the formation of the HKVDC. The Mobile Machine Gun Company had no role to perform in the new scheme, and the members of that unit were consequently transferred to Nos 1 and 2 companies.

The mainland forces, under the command of Brigadier C. Wallis, were as follows: the 2nd Battalion Royal Scots (Lieut-Colonel S. M. White, MC) held the left sector from the Texaco Peninsula to the Shing Mun Redoubt; the 2/14 Punjabis (Lieut-Colonel G. R. Kidd) were in the centre, and the 5/7 Rajputs (Lieut-Colonel J. Cadogan-Rawlinson) were on the right, the end of the line being the sea near Shatin railway-station. Owing to the extensive front, each battalion's lay-out consisted of a line of platoon localities, the gaps between which were covered by fire by day and by patrolling at night. One company only of each battalion could be kept in reserve, and this was normally located in a prepared position covering the most dangerous line of enemy approach. The reserve company of the centre battalion (2/14 Punjabis) was employed initially as "Forward Troops" on the Taipo Road to cover the demolition parties and to delay the enemy's advance.

The Field Company Engineers of the HKVDC, under Major J. H. Bottomley, were responsible for the demolitions on road and railway from Fanling back to Shatin, and were consequently also in the forward area; as also were HKVDC Armoured Cars, under 2/Lieut M. G. Carruthers. No 1 Company HKVDC (Captain A. H. Penn) was at Kai Tak airfield, acting as local protection and as reserve for the Gin-Drinkers Line. One platoon of No 1 Company had recently been equipped with Carriers, and this platoon, under 2/Lieut R. Edwards, was patrolling the Castle Peak Road. Mainland artillery comprised one troop of 6 inch Howitzers, one of 4.5 inch Howitzers, and two troops of 3.7 inch Howitzers.

On the island were the 1st Battalion Middlesex (Lieut-Colonel H. W. M. Stewart, OBE, MC); the 1st Battalion Winnipeg Grenadiers (Lieut-Colonel J. L. R. Sutcliffe) and the 1st Battalion Royal Rifles of Canada (Lieut Colonel W. J. Home). The HKVDC units on the island, under Colonel H. B. Rose, MC, comprised four batteries and one AA battery; three rifle companies, three machine-gun companies, one LMG anti-aircraft company; Corps and Fortress Signals; the Field Ambulance Company, the ASC Company; Supply and Transport Section; Pay Detachment; the Stanley Platoon, the Special Guard Company, the Hughes Group, or "hughesiliers" (Home Guardsmen who were later to make themselves famous); and the Nursing Detachment.

The Island Commander was Brigadier J. K. Lawson, MC, of the Canadians.

It was unfortunate that neither the Royal Scots nor the Rajputs had sufficient time to become acquainted with their battle positions. In fact, of our six infantry battalions only two knew their roles in detail - the Middlesex, who were on beach defence on the south and west of the island, and the Punjabis who had throughout been "Mainland Troops". The Canadians, who only arrived in the Colony on November 16th, had no time even to become acclimatized, much less to learn the peculiar geographical features of the country. Another month or two would have made a vast difference.

The Opening Phase

During the first few days of December, the political situation became critical. By December 7th all troops were in their battle positions. Major Gray[1] with the Forward Troops was at Fanling, maintaining frontier observation posts. With him was 2/Lieut I. B. Tamworth with a demolition party of HKVDC Engineers.

At 0445 hours on December 8th, our Intelligence picked up a Tokyo broadcast giving code instructions to Japanese nationals that war with Great Britain and the USA was imminent. Word was at once sent to Major Gray, and orders given that the forward demolitions should be exploded.

---

[1] Major G. Gray, Punjabis

By 0645 the garrison had been warned that the British Empire and Japan were at war; but to the vast majority of the civilian population the first intimation came at 0800 hours when Japanese aircraft attacked Kai Tak airfield and damaged or destroyed five RAF and eight civil planes, thus putting our entire air force out of action. Shamshuipo barracks were also attacked, but there were few casualties, the troops having already deployed.

At 0800 hours our observation posts beyond Fanling reported that enemy troops were crossing into Laffan's Plain by the hundred. The force there was estimated at a battalion, and later information showed that this advance force attacked on a two-battalion front, one making across country by way of Laffan's Plain, the other using the Taipo Road.

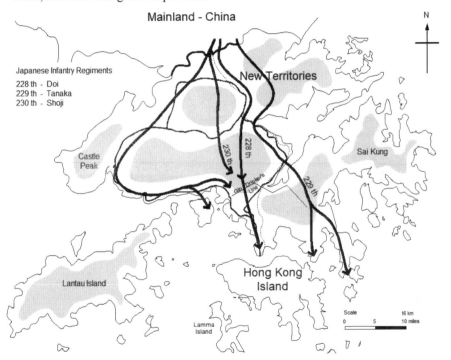

Japanese Advance on the Mainland

Opinions varied as to the strength of the Japanese forces. It is now known that Lieut-General Sakai used two divisions, with a third in reserve. The strength of the division which later landed on the island was given by the infantry commander, Lieut-General (then Major-General) Ito Takeo, at rather more than 20,000 men, and we can assume that the total Japanese force was about 60,000 men.

In accordance with his instructions, Lieut Tamworth destroyed two bridges at Lowu, completing the demolition by 0830 hours. While doing this, he and his party were within easy rifle range of the Japanese sappers who were constructing a bridge over the Shumchun River. Tamworth then withdrew to Gill's Cutting, where four mines had previously been prepared. By arrangement with Major Gray, and after all transport had been withdrawn, Tamworth exploded the mines and established blocks on the road and railway. He then withdrew his party to Taipo Market, where Major Bottomley was waiting.

Meanwhile the Punjabis were slowly withdrawing. The Japanese battalion moving down the Taipo Road was a constant menace to their left flank, and Major Gray decided not to attempt any delaying action until he had made sure of the two main demolitions, No 731 and R 34, about a mile north of Taipo.

Here Captain K. S. Robertson had prepared three more bridges for demolition and, on the visible approach of the enemy, at about 1200 hours, these demolitions were carried out successfully. After destroying petrol pumps in Taipo Market, the Field Company withdrew with the Punjabis to a line running inland from the north side of Taipo Causeway.

It was on this line that Major Gray decided to stand, and soon after 1500 hours the Japanese advance party attacked and was driven off. A platoon of Punjabis had been posted wide on the left as a flank guard. At 1830 hours an enemy detachment, led by three Chinese guides, walked into the ambush, and practically the whole detachment was wiped out. At about 1900 hours the Armoured Cars participated in another ambush, when a Japanese platoon, moving down the road in close formation, was annihilated.

The Japanese then commenced outflanking tactics, sending patrols through the hills, and Major Gray withdrew his troops south of the Taipo Causeway. Meanwhile Major Bottomley's men had prepared three more demolitions, which were exploded successfully; Forward Troops then withdrew to the vicinity of Cheung Shiu Tan.

The Japanese advance during the day had been rapid, but there was no slackening off after nightfall. The enemy continued to press forward in small parties, led by guides who knew the least-frequented paths over the hills, and the Punjabis were continually in danger of being outflanked. At 2030 hours Captain Robertson blew up the railway tunnel. The explosion unfortunately destroyed Major Gray's communications with his left flank platoon, under Lieut Blair, and it was necessary to put a time-table into operation. The Japanese continued their outflanking movements, and Major Gray decided on another withdrawal. At 2200 hours and 2230 hours the next two road-bridges were destroyed. At the second of these Captain F. A. Redmond had provided two circuits-one an electrical one, one a time-fuse. Sgt R. J. V. Everest lit the time fuse, but some of the Japanese advance party were on his heels and they cut the fuse. They were presumably congratulating themselves upon having saved the bridge when the electrical circuit was completed and bridge and Japanese went up together.

At midnight Forward Troops were at Taipo Mai, but enemy patrols were soon again threatening the left flank and at 0100 hours on the 9th a further withdrawal was made to the Fo Tan Valley.

At 0200 hours Field Company Engineers were withdrawn to Kowloon Railway Station, leaving two demolition parties near Kowloon Reservoir. Major Bottomley reported that all demolitions had been successfully carried out along the Taipo Road.

On the other route, the Castle Peak Road, where the enemy did not appear, all demolitions were successful, except at the Dairy Farm, where a daring saboteur slipped in after the covering party had withdrawn, and cut the leads. He was killed while trying to repeat this feat at the next demolition.

At dawn on the 9th, the Punjabis were on Tau Fung Shan Monastery Ridge, near Shatin, their last point of withdrawal before reaching the Line. Here they had artillery support as well as full co-operation of the Armoured Cars. During the day the Japanese offered a number of excellent targets for the artillery. At 1800 hours Major Gray withdrew his men to the Gin-Drinkers Line. Forward Troops carried out their role excellently and inflicted heavy loss on the enemy.

The Mainland Battle

Throughout the afternoon of December 9th, enemy patrols were active along our front. In the left sector, on the tracks leading south from the Kam Tin area, men of the Royal Scots had several encounters with the enemy, and confirmed that their patrols were in many cases led by local guides. The enemy scouts and snipers were well trained and knew their work. They carried small camouflage nets rolled on their shoulders and their quilted uniforms were designed for the insertion of grass and twigs.

Now that the fighting had come near Kowloon, arrangements were made during the night for the evacuation of Chinese villagers from places near the battle area. Also at 2200 hours the last CNAC planes left Kai Tak aerodrome for Free China. With them went Lieut-Colonel H. Owen Hughes, HKVDC, who was to act as liaison officer with the 7th Chinese Military Zone.

The Shingmun Redoubt

As can be seen on the map, the longest part of the line, that extending from Texaco Peninsula to Shingmun Redoubt was also the most vulnerable. It was held by the Royal Scots; 'A' Company being on the right, with a platoon occupying the redoubt; 'B' and 'C' companies holding the centre and left, with 'D' Company in reserve. It was expected that the redoubt would effectually prevent any enemy penetration into the Shingmun river valley. During the early part of the night there was much enemy activity along our front, chiefly against the Punjabis' position. The Punjabis' line was very thin, where it joined with the Royal Scots line at Shingmun, and Brigadier Wallis moved the reserve company of the Rajputs (under Captain H. R. Newton) across to strengthen this weak spot.

Soon after 2300 hours Captain Newton reported that Japanese were moving down the Shingmun Valley, below the reservoir, across his front. 'A' Company Royal Scots reported having heard explosions from the direction of the redoubt, and heavy enemy pressure in the Pineapple Pass area. Within an hour it became all too clear that the redoubt, together with the artillery observation post, had fallen into enemy hands at the very first onset.

This was a major disaster, for the redoubt was the key position to the left sector, and its loss endangered the whole of the left flank, and indeed the whole of the Gin-Drinkers Line. 'B' and 'C' Companies Royal Scots, positioned on the Texaco Peninsula and on the road leading from Tsun Wan to Pineapple Pass, now had their right flank exposed.

During the remainder of the night there was confused fighting in the Shingmun Valley, where the Rajputs finally hustled the Japanese back past the reservoir and into the redoubt. A proposal was made by Lieut-Colonel Kidd for an immediate counter-attack on the redoubt, but this was ruled out on the grounds that the nearest troops that could be spared were a mile away, that the ground was rugged and precipitous and the enemy at the redoubt probably far superior numerically to any force we could bring against them without seriously weakening other parts of our line.

As the line appeared to be weakest in the area immediately west of the redoubt, 'D' Company Royal Scots (Captain D. Pinkerton), which had been acting as reserve company, was put in on the left of 'A' Company. As a further reinforcement, the reserve company of the Winnipeg Grenadiers was brought across the harbour and stationed at the junction of the Taipo and Castle Peak roads.

At about 0930 hours on the 10th the enemy pushed forward in force from the Shingmun Redoubt. The Rajputs engaged them and with artillery support, drove them back with, as Captain Newton reported, heavy losses. A proposal was made that Captain Newton's company should follow up their success and make a counterattack on the redoubt, while the enemy in that area were, demoralised. A forward movement of the company, however, would have left a wide gap on the left of the Punjabis' position; and the Japanese were already pressing attacks all along the Punjabis' front, and trying to infiltrate. By midday Newton's company and 'A' and 'D' Companies Royal Scots were fully occupied in repelling attacks as the Japanese patrols sought to exploit their success and force a passage between our Centre and Left Sectors.

It was fortunate for us that the demolition of the bridge near Au Tau on the Castle Peak Road prevented the enemy from getting any of their transport past that point. The Japanese managed to get a tractor-drawn battery of 5.9 Howitzers on to the Kam Tin aerodrome, and this battery bombarded Stonecutters Island and Mount Davis consistently. Attempts to remove the demolitions on the Castle Peak Road were prevented by HMS Cicala, gunboat, which was covering the left flank of the Royal Scots, and which successfully broke up every attempt of Japanese working parties to repair the damage to the road. The little gunboat also did splendid service in bringing flanking fire to bear on enemy troops pressing forward to attack the front held by 'B' and 'C' Companies Royal Scots - the Pineapple Pass track. At about 1500 hours Japanese aircraft commenced vigorous attacks, and though their dive-bombing on that occasion was most inaccurate, the gunboat had little chance. At about 1615 hours she received a hit which necessitated her going to Aberdeen for repairs.

It having been decided that any attempt to recapture the Shingmun Redoubt was out of the question, it was vitally necessary to alter the line and to withdraw 'B' and 'C' Companies Royal Scots from their exposed position.

This was done after dark. The troops withdrew quietly; the enemy, though actually in contact with them, not realising that any movement was being carried out, and the withdrawal was completed without incident though "the two companies required a certain amount of adjustment before dawn." The new line ran from the south end of the Shingmun Reservoir through Golden Hill to Laichikok, and was the weakest part of our defence, as it included the Pass west of Golden Hill, which was regarded as one of the two "very vulnerable features."

The Battle of Golden Hill

During the early hours of the 11th, the Japanese patrols, feeling their way forwards, came into contact with our men on the left of Golden Hill. During the remainder of the night they were busy bringing up their reserves and infiltrating in small parties through the very thin line of defence. The attack came at dawn all along the line held by 'B' and 'C' companies. By 0700 hours the enemy had occupied Golden Hill. The two companies of Royal Scots were absolutely overwhelmed by superior numbers. Both company commanders were killed and more than sixty of the men were casualties. The remainder fell back in considerable confusion but were not overrun. A complete disaster was prevented by the vigorous action of 'D' Company, stationed on the right of Golden Hill. These counter-attacked the enemy and succeeded in regaining possession of the hill and, though they were unable to hold it in face of the large numbers of the enemy attacking, they were able to keep possession long enough for the remainder of 'B' Company to extricate itself from what might have been a complete trap. Carruthers' armoured cars and Edwards' carriers were rushed forward along the Castle Peak Road and covered the retreat of 'C' Company, while the Reserve Company Winnipeg Grenadiers was moved forward towards Laichikok.

These measures checked any further Japanese forward movement in the area; though, considering their numbers - it was estimated that the attacking force was two battalions - the pause in the attack seems strange. Actually for the remainder of the day, the enemy made no further attempt to push forward in the Laichikok area, though there was considerable activity along the front of the Rajputs, particularly around Shatin station area.

The situation, from our point of view, was sufficiently depressing. The enemy, by holding Golden Hill, could command the road junction and a considerable part of the Taipo Road, and this endangered all the units which were using the Taipo Road as a line of supply; namely, the Punjabis, one company of the Rajputs and two Howitzer Troops.

The Withdrawal from the Mainland

December 11th

These two disasters made it impossible for us to hold the Gin-Drinkers Line; indeed, west of the Shingmun Valley, held by Newton's Rajputs, there was no line. The Royal Scots, one company of Grenadiers, a platoon of No 1 Company HKVDC, the Carrier Platoon and two Armoured Cars were extended obliquely back almost to Shamshuipo. At midday orders were given for a withdrawal of all troops under cover of night; the Rajputs and Punjabis were to retire to Devil's Peak, the remainder to Kowloon Peninsula, where they would embark for the island.

As soon as orders for the withdrawal were given out, the HKVDC Field Company Engineers began to get busy. Lieut Tamworth with Sgt Palmer and a party carried out demolition work at the Cement Works and the China Light and Power. Personnel of the Dock Company thoroughly demolished the docks. The Field Company also had the task of salving as much transport as possible, and vehicles of all kinds were rushed to the Vehicular Ferry. No 1 Company HKVDC also had an arduous task. One platoon was already in action near Laichikok; a second was manning the carriers; and the remainder had to guard against a surprise attack on the aerodrome, cover the withdrawal of troops being evacuated from the east side of the peninsula, deal with Fifth Columnists, looters and rioters, and finally complete the demolition of the aerodrome.

The withdrawal of three battalions from their forward position was a most difficult and hazardous operation. There had been no previous practice for want of time; the night was exceedingly dark; the troops had to break off contact with the enemy and move, in some cases, across the front of the advancing Japanese. The two battalions on the right flank had the hardest task. The Rajputs, followed by the Punjabis, moved along the line of the Passes - Kowloon Pass, Shatin Pass, Grasscutters Pass - to Devil's Peak.

This would have been a strenuous march for light-armed troops in daylight. The two Indian battalions were carrying all their stores and equipment and the night was exceptionally dark, rendering progress along the hill tracks slow and laborious. In addition, the Punjabis in the rear were in close contact with the enemy, and for much of the march, were actually fighting a rear-guard action. It was a remarkable feat that both battalions arrived at Devil's Peak, not only intact, but without losing any of their military stores.

In comparison the Royal Scots and the one company of Grenadiers had an easy task. They retired towards Shamshuipo and Mongkok, covered by the Carriers and the Armoured Cars, and were taken across in launches and ferry-boats. When all had been evacuated - just before midnight - the armoured cars, less one, which had been knocked out, and the carriers were shipped across on the vehicular ferry-boat. On the other side of the peninsula, No 1 Company HKVDC completed the demolitions at the aerodrome and then withdrew from Kowloon City Pier using the R.A.F. launch.

The troops on Stonecutters Island were withdrawn by ferry-boat during the same night. These comprised a battery of the HKSRA, under Major Mills, two platoons of No 3 Company HKVDC (Major E. G. Stewart) and some RE details. The island had been shelled and bombed consistently for three days and practically every building had been hit, but the casualties had been surprisingly small. No 3 Company had only lost four men wounded, Cpl F. E. C. C. Quah and three Other Ranks.

The evacuation was carried out successfully, all stores removed as far as was possible, and the remainder, together with the wireless installations, demolished before the troops embarked. Unfortunately, soon after the troops had disembarked at the naval yard, the ferry-boat was sunk, and all stores and kit were lost.

While these withdrawals were proceeding satisfactorily, the Rajputs and Punjabis were continuing their arduous march on Devil's Peak. The Punjabis were unable to carry out the timed programme for the withdrawal, but through no fault of their own. The re,arguard, comprising part of HQ Company, under Lieut Forsyth, was cut off from the main body at Shatin Pass, and so withdrew down the road to Kowloon City, where they became involved in fighting with Fifth

Columnists as well as with advancing Japanese patrols. With Pte B. A. Gellman of No 1 Company HKVDC acting as guide the Punjabis made their way through the streets of the town to the Star Ferry Wharf. Conditions in Kowloon at this time were far from pleasant; on the withdrawal of the civil police, rioting and looting had broken out; shops and houses were being looted and Fifth Columnists were busy sniping any of our troops who could be attacked. At the Star Ferry, Forsyth took over charge from the police and for the remainder of the night the Punjabis guarded the wharf and assisted refugees onto the ferries, which ran continuously. Soon after dawn the advance partly of the Japanese appeared and occupied Kowloon Railway Station. A military police in Salisbury Road adjured the advance party of Japanese to "double up there and get a move on". Then, realising his mistake, he obeyed his own injunction. The Punjabis engaged them for some time, but on the approach of the main body of the enemy at about 1000 hours, Forsyth embarked his men on the last ferry-boat, which left the wharf with light automatics and rifles firing from her stern. An RAMC Orderly, wounded in the neck, unable to reach the wharf, swam across the harbour - no mean feat in such cold water. A Punjabi signaller, similarly cut off and unable to swim, made his way across the harbour in a life-belt.

Two other companies of Punjabis, delayed by enemy action, did not reach Devil's Peak until long after daybreak. Meanwhile the Rajputs, who had arrived first, manned the Ma Lau Tong Line, with one troop of 3.7 Howitzers in support.

The Island Battle

The Period of Waiting

Already by December 10th the Japanese had shown signs of activity in the near vicinity of the island. On the morning of the 11th the enemy made a landing on Lamma Island and our guns at Jubilee Fort and Aberdeen went into action against them. During the afternoon of the same way a party of Japanese in sampans tried to make a surprise landing on Aberdeen Island, occupied by 3rd Battery HKVDC (Captain C. W. L. Cole) and a platoon of Winnipeg Grenadiers. The attack was repulsed by machine-gun fire. Later still, a concentration of about a hundred junks was seen off Lamma, and these were engaged by our artillery. On the 12th the Japanese were seen to be occupying George Island, near Lamma, and there was considerable activity in that vicinity. This constant menace of a surprise landing on the west or south-west of the island enforced us to keep troops on beach defence all along the threatened coast-line.

Evacuation from Devil's Peak

December 12th

Throughout the day air raids and shelling of the island continued, chiefly along the North Shore

On the mainland the Ma Lau Tong Line was bombed continuously, and at about 1700 hours an attack was launched on the left of the line. The enemy was about one battalion strong, and the attack was repulsed with considerable loss to the Japanese. Other attacks developed along the line, equally unsuccessful, and there was heavy bombing and mortar fire. It was decided to evacuate the position and concentrate all troops on the island.

After nightfall the evacuation began and proved even more hazardous than the previous one. Launch crews deserted and many launches had been damaged by enemy fire and were unserviceable. Officers from HQ were sent down to accelerate matters and these took personal charge of launches, manned in many cases by volunteer crews. The old WDV Victoria, under charge of Major A. J. Dewar and Captain C. G. Turner[2], did excellent work. By 0130 hours on the 13th the Punjabis had all been evacuated. By 0400 hours most of the 1st Troop RA and one company of Rajputs were across, though the mules had to be left behind. The tide was now out, which necessitated the men being ferried out by sampan, and as daylight was not far off the situation was critical. The Royal Navy was then called on to assist and responded nobly. Three MTBs were sent from Aberdeen and a fourth, which had been covering the right flank of the Ma Lau Tong Line, was also called in. HMS Thracian also arrived from Aberdeen. Despite all difficulties the evacuation proceeded rapidly. 'A' and 'C' Companies of the Rajputs were holding the second and shorter of the Lines, the Hai Wan Line. These troops were in close contact with the enemy and a withdrawal was no easy matter. Fortunately the rough handling which the enemy had experienced a few hours earlier had discouraged them from any attack in force. One company covered the withdrawal of the other, and then retired as rapidly as possible. Daylight had come and the operations were clearly visible to the enemy but the last men reached "Thracian" safely and were taken to Aberdeen.

While the last contingent of the Rajputs was still in transit, Lieut-General Sakai sent over a flag of truce with a letter to HE the Governor. The letter made demands tantamount to unconditional surrender and threatened that, in the event of a refusal, the town and island would be subjected to heavy artillery and aerial bombardment. The demand was rejected categorically.

---

[2] Both RASC

In expectation of an attack on the island, certain preparations were made which could not have been done during peace time. In these the Field Company HKVDC took a prominent part. The Hong Kong Engineering Corps was formed, and Major J. Smith (HKVDC) established depots at Happy Valley, Kennedy Town, Pokfulam, Repulse Bay and Stanley. Unfortunately the recruitment did not come up to expectation, in fact, barely 200 workers were available. The Corps, under the command of Major Bottomley, in the absence of Lieut-Colonel R. D. Walker, MC, who was ill, carried out a considerable amount of work during the next few days. The whole front from Shaukiwan to Kennedy Town was wired, sheds at North Point were destroyed and gun bases, were constructed in the Naval Yard.

December 13th

During the day artillery fire was intensified. One of the 9.2 guns on Mount Davis received a direct hit and was knocked out. 4th Battery HKVDC (Lieut K. M. A. Barnett) at Pak Sha Wan was specially singled out for attention. Belcher's Fort was set on fire and other serious fires were started in Kennedy Town and West Point. By midnight further fires had developed, and the Fire Brigade, which had been hard at work for many hours, asked for military assistance. The fires were finally got under control by midday on the 14th, but they had a very disturbing effect on civilian morale.

December 14th

Shelling was equally heavy on this day. Two guns at Belcher's Fort were put out of action and an AA Battery at Mount Davis was completely wrecked. 4th Battery HKVDC was again pounded - the BC Post and all internal communications being destroyed. Lieut Barnett was wounded and went to hospital and, through some extraordinary error, the Chinese personnel of the Battery were sent to Stanley. Their place, however, was filled by a few British gunners and 2/Lieut Sleap took over command until Barnett's return.

The new organisation was now completed and the island was divided into two Brigade areas. West Brigade (Brigadier J. K. Lawson, MC) comprised the Middlesex, Royal Scots, the Punjab Regiment. The Punjabis were holding the shore-line from the Naval Yard westwards to Telegraph Bay; the Middlesex carried on from that point to Stanley peninsula, and were also responsible for the coast between Causeway Bay and the Naval Yard. The Royal Scots were in the area around Happy Valley. Brigade HQ was on the road 100 yards West of Wongneichong Gap. East Brigade (Brigadier C. Wallis) comprised the Rajputs, the Grenadiers and the Royal Rifles. The Rajputs held the coast-line from Causeway Bay eastwards to Sai Wan; the Royal Rifles were mainly along the coast from that point to Stanley; and the Grenadiers were in the Repulse Bay

Deepwater Bay area. Brigade HQ was at the point where the Shek-O Road joins Island Road - overlooking Saiwan.

After hostilities began on the island, the Grenadiers were attached to West Brigade.

The HKVDC units were positioned as follows:-

1st Battery (Captain G. F. Rees) Cape D'Aguilar.

2nd Battery (Captain D. J. S. Crozier) Bluff Head, Stanley.

3rd Battery (Captain C. W. L. Cole) Aberdeen Island.

4th Battery (Lieut K. M. A. Barnett) Pak Sha Wan.

5th Battery (Capt. L. Goldman) Sai Wan Hill.

Field Company Engineers (Major J. H. Bottomley) HQ at Tai Hang.

Corps Signals (Captain A. N. Braude) HQ at Peak Mansions.

Armoured Car Platoon (2/Lieut M. G. Carruthers) HQ at West Brigade HQ

No 1 Company (Capt A. H. Penn) Tytam Valley.

No 2 Company (Major H. R. Forsyth) Pottinger Gap and Big Wave Bay.

No 3 Company (Major E. G. Stewart) Jardine's Look-out.

No 4 Company (Captain R. K. Valentine) High West, Victoria Gap and Mount Kellett.

No 5 Company (Captain C. A. D'Almada) Mount Davis.

No 6 Company (Captain H. A. de B. Botelho) The North Shore.

No 7 Company (Captain J. G. B. Dewar) Magazine Gap, Wanchai Gap, Middle Gap.

ASC Company (Major F. Flippance) HQ Deepwater Bay.

Hughes Group (Major the Hon. J. J. Paterson) North Point Power Station.

The Supply and Transport Section (Major H. G. Williams) was attached to HKVDC, HQ, which had moved on the 14th from Garden Road to Peak Mansions. The Field Ambulance Company (Lieut-Colonel L. T. Ride) was widely distributed. The Pay Detachment (Major C. de S. Robertson, MM) was attached to Royal Army Pay Corps. The Nursing Detachment (Mrs. Braude) was attached to Army Hospitals.

The Attempted Landing

December 15th

Throughout the day there was systematic shelling of the pillboxes along the North Shore, held by 'C' and 'D' Companies of the Rajputs. Three were completely demolished and two others were badly damaged. The most accurate fire came from a high-velocity small-calibre gun hidden in one of the Kowloon godowns. Aberdeen and Sai Wan were also shelled.

During the day a "Command Observation Post" manned by men from the HKVDC Signals, was established on the Peak. This operated well, although the OP was forced to move several times as, despite every precaution, enemy artillery continued to find it and put down heavy concentrations.

Later in the day a collection of craft was seen in Kowloon Bay. Concentrated fire by the 6 inch Howitzers set two craft alight; the remainder scattered. In expectation of a raid that night, orders were given that in the event of machine-gun fire being heard from the North Shore, searchlights should be depressed to illuminate the harbour.

At 2115 hours, No 2 Platoon, Royal Rifles, opened fire from West Fort, Pak Sha Wan. The No 2 searchlight of 4th Battery HKVDC was depressed and showed Japanese in considerable numbers crossing the Channel, using a junk, small rafts and rubber boats. The battery promptly opened fire and sank the junk, besides doing considerable damage among the rafts. The small-arms fire of the Canadians apparently accounted for the remainder. The Japanese counter-batteries quickly opened with howitzer and 3 pdr fire; the searchlight was hit and considerable further damage done to the fort. Again, at about 2245 hours, the enemy was observed to be attempting a crossing from San Tong and Sam Ki Tsun Bays. Fire was opened by aid of the West Fort fixed beam and the North Shore Lyon Light. 2/Lieut Sleap reported four enemy craft sunk.

For its prompt action the depleted 4th Battery was commended.

Later that night HMS Thracian carried out a daring raid. She made her way from Aberdeen across the enemy front on the peninsula to Kowloon Bay where she sank two ferry-boats filled with troops.

December 16th

There was again heavy shelling of the North Shore. There were also numerous air-raids during the day on Mount Davis, Shek-O, Lyemun and Aberdeen, where HMS Thracian was hit, causing casualties. The shelling continued throughout the night and there was also heavy long-range mortar fire on to the North Shore, where more pill-boxes were damaged.

December 17th

At dawn there was a mass air-raid, followed by a heavy bombardment. Lieut-General Sakai then sent another flag of truce with proposals similar to the previous ones. He added a hint that rejection would mean a more intensive and less discriminating bombardment. Hostilities were suspended until 1600 hours; after which the bombardment recommenced. The Field Company Engineers at Tai Hang received a considerable share of this and orders were given for their HQ to be moved to Repulse Bay.

December 18th

There was again heavy shelling of the North Shore, but our counter-batteries were at last able to hit back vigorously, and they silenced the enemy's guns on Devil's Peak, at Gun Club Hill and on the water-front.

The morale of the troops was good but the strain of waiting for the inevitable enemy landing was not pleasant. It appeared as if the Japanese were none too eager to make the attempt; at least, not until the North Shore defences had been "softened" by their artillery and bombing attacks. This delay was all to the good for us, for every day was of value. Hong Kong was fulfilling its role as "an outpost of empire", since the duty of an outpost is to delay the enemy and inflict as much damage as possible before being overrun.

The Landing

December 18th / 19th

For the attack on the island, Lieut-General Sakai brought up the 38th Division, which had been in reserve during the fighting on the mainland. This division was commanded by Lieut-General Sano, but the actual operations on the island were entrusted to the infantry commander, Major-General Ito Takeo. The three infantry regiments of the 38th division were commanded by Colonel Doi, Colonel Tanaka Ryosabura and Colonel Shoji Toshishige.

After the war, in March and April 1947, three of these commanders, Lieut-General Ito and Major-Generals Tanaka and Shoji, were tried in Hong Kong for atrocities committed by the troops under their command during the period of hostilities. Their war-diaries were produced in evidence. We thus have a clear account of the enemy forces and of the progress of the battle as seen from the Japanese side.

From these accounts it appears that the 38th Division was composed as follows:-

The Right Flank Group. This was under the direct command of Major-General Ito and consisted of two battalions of the 228th (Colonel Doi) and all three battalions of the 230th Regiment (Colonel Shoji), with other details.

The Left Flank Group. This was acting independently under the command of Colonel Tanaka. It consisted of two battalions of the 229th Regiment, with other details.

The Divisional Reserve Infantry. This was two battalions; one from the 228th and one from the 229th.

The Right Artillery Group. This apparently included at least one Mountain Battery.

The Left Artillery Group.

The Kowloon Garrison Force. Strength and composition not known, but apparently composed of "garrison" or second-line battalions.

An Armoured Unit; light tanks.

Engineers, Signals, Supply and Transport, etc.

The total strength of the division was given at rather more than 20,000 men.

A Japanese infantry regiment (Rentai) normally consisted of three battalions (Daitai), and each battalion was larger than one of ours, as it usually comprised a HQ company, a machine-gun company and four rifle companies. General Ito gave the strength of each infantry battalion (which included an unspecified number of gendarmerie) at 1,100 men. The whole force which landed on the island on the night of December 18/19 was seven battalions, or rather more than 7,500 men. These were landed in two waves, timed for 2030 hours and 2230 hours.

On the 19th the Divisional Reserve and both artillery groups were brought over, and later, as resistance on the island proved to be stronger, and the Japanese losses considerably greater than had been anticipated, more troops were brought across from the other two divisions. It appears that three more Rentais (nine infantry battalions) were brought over, together with some artillery and some "garrison" battalions.

The attack came on the front from North Point to Lyemun and three separate landings were made. Colonel Tanaka with the 229th, acting independently, took the left or east flank; Colonel Doi, with the 228th, the centre; Colonel Shoji and the 230th, the right or west flank. Tanaka's men landed at Shaukiwan. Their task was twofold - to occupy Lyemun and Sai Wan, and to force a way into Taitam Valley, either over Mount Parker or through Quarry Gap. They landed in two waves; the first battalion to land was sent against Lyemun, the second against Quarry Gap. Both battalions were to rendezvous in Taitam Valley.

The 230th landed in the neighbourhood of North Point, also in two waves, and moved straight inland towards Jardine's Look-out and Wongneichong Gap, which was their principal objective. They apparently moved across country until they reached Sir Cecil's Ride.

Colonel Doi's men landed west of the Docks. Their task was to take care of the bridge-head and, when possible, push troops forward to support the 230th. Doi and Shoji were to rendezvous somewhere in the vicinity of Wongneichong Gap.

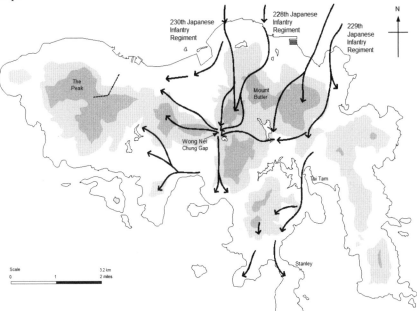

Japanese Advance on the Island

Orders seem to have been somewhat vague and it is not surprising that Major-General Ito reported that he lost touch with all three units for twenty-four hours. Shoji also spoke feelingly of "the dense fog" which obscured the landscape on the morning of the 19th. The fog was mainly mental, and Shoji was by no means the only sufferer.

The night of December 18/19 was exceptionally dark; the sky was overcast and there were frequent showers of rain. In addition the Japanese artillery fire had set fire to the oil tanks near North Point, and the strong wind brought the smoke in a dense pall over the northern part of the island. The result was darkness almost impenetrable. This, we are told, handicapped the Japanese, but was much worse for the defending force, whose effective field of fire was reduced to a few yards. As one man later expressed it, "You couldn't see a Jap at the end of your bayonet."

Lyemun and Sai Wan

Tanaka's men carried out their task well. The first battalion landed on time, overrun No 2 Platoon of the Royal Rifles, captured Lyemun Barracks and the 6 inch Howitzer Battery there, and at 2130 hours attacked the much battered 4th Battery at Pak Sha Wan. No 1 gun was overrun, but the enemy did not press the attack. Lieut H. T. Buxton, believing the fort to be in enemy hands, collected what men he could and withdrew towards Lyemun Barracks, hoping to join with the Canadians there. The party was ambushed and Buxton was killed. Meanwhile the sentry on No 2 gun was reporting to Lieut Barnett that "nothing unusual had occurred." Barnett thought otherwise and, with the nine remaining gunners, opened fire on Shaukiwan, where he guessed correctly that the enemy was landing.

For some unknown reason, the Japanese made no further attempts to capture the fort, which was completely isolated. On the morning of the 20th, Barnett's party was joined by the survivors of a platoon of 'A' Company, Rajputs, from West Fort. On the 21st, the position being hopeless, Barnett surrendered.

These men of the Tanaka Butai were tough and seasoned fighters, and, as will be seen, they were given a large share of the fighting on the island. They were also the most ruthless and were responsible for most of the atrocities committed during the fighting. At about 2230 hours they overran the 5th (AA) Battery HKVDC at Sai Wan Hill, the gunners being still unaware that a landing had taken place. Half-a-dozen were bayoneted, some thirty escaped and twenty were taken prisoner. These were tied up and kept in confinement for some hours. They were then taken out and bayoneted, and their bodies were thrown over the wall. Two Volunteers, Bdr Martin Tso Hin-chi and Pte Chan Yam Kwong (Medical Section) were left for dead, but managed to crawl away later.

The Salesian Mission at Shaukiwan was being used as an Advanced Dressing Station, manned by Canadian and British medical personnel, under Major S. M. Bamfill (RCAMC). When the Japanese arrived there, they first murdered two wounded officers of the Rajputs, who were being brought in by ambulance; then they confined the doctors and orderlies in one room for several hours. In the early hours of the morning of the 19th, the prisoners were taken outside, stripped, lined up along the side of the nullah and bayoneted amidst shouts of laughter from the Japanese onlookers. Three men, Major Bamfill, Dr O. Thomas and one orderly, had miraculous escapes.

The only point that can be quoted in favour of Tanaka's butchers is that they did not harm the women; the nurses, VADs and members of St John Ambulance; and that they were not so bestial as the men who later perpetrated the massacre at St Stephen's Hospital.

The Hughesiliers at the Power Station

Meanwhile the troops forming the first wave of the Doi and Shoji Butais were making their way onshore between North Point and the Docks. Scarcely a pill-box remained undamaged and the thin line of Rajputs, 'C' and 'D' Companies only, could not hold the massed attack. Once ashore, as has been said, Shoji's men pressed straight on inland, leaving Doi's men to do the "mopping up".

It was apparently Doi's men, therefore, who were responsible for the first of the atrocities on the island, when a number of members of St John's Ambulance Brigade and ARP workers were arrested and later executed, mostly by beheading.

The Japanese quickly captured the Sugar Factory, and 'C' Company was overrun, though a few section posts continued to hold out for some hours. Further west, Captain Newton with part of 'D' Company put up a strong resistance, though Newton himself was killed. At the Power Station the enemy came up against the "Hughesiliers". These veterans found themselves acting as front-line troops, in which role they acquitted themselves right nobly.

As a counter-attack, 'B' Company Rajputs, under Captain R. G. Course, moved in from the west side, striking towards Tai Hang, where they hoped to join up with some survivors of 'D' Company. 2/Lieut Carruthers took an Armoured Car along King's Road in a gallant attempt to reach the Power Station; a platoon of Middlesex followed behind. The Armoured Car was knocked out by a direct hit from a mobile anti-tank gun, and Carruthers was the only man not hit. The Middlesex platoon came under the same fire and half the men were shot down. Most of the survivors managed to reach the Power Station, where they did splendid work.

At 0145 hours Major Paterson reported that the Power Station was entirely surrounded by the enemy. He was ordered to hold on as long as possible in order to assist any other units which might be resisting in the area. Also it was hoped that 'B' Company Rajputs would soon be able to strike in that direction.

'B' Company did make some considerable headway; one platoon penetrated as far as Braemar Point, and was joined there by the survivors of 'D' Company - thirty-five men, all the officers having been killed. The Rajputs could not hold their ground, however, much less move towards the Power Station, and at about 0230 hours the Company withdrew to a position north-east of Leighton

Hill. Units of the Middlesex holding two pill-boxes in Causeway Bay, tried to connect up with the Power Station, but this attempt also failed.

Major Paterson and his men, thus isolated, made one of the finest defences of the whole battle. They held the Power Station throughout the night; and, when driven out, continued house-to-house fighting. A party of a dozen Middlesex and Volunteers held the main office building until it burned over their heads. Part of the fighting centred round a derelict omnibus in King's Road, the so-called "Battle of the Bus". It was here that Pte T. E. ("Tam") Pearce told Paterson that he would as soon be killed under a bus as roasted alive inside a burning building, and "at the time there seemed to be quite a bit in what he said - not much choice either way". It was here too that after Cpl R. P. Dunlop and Ptes V. Sorby, Pearce and J. Roscoe had become casualties, the last man, Pte G. E. Gahagan, drove off an enemy patrol single-handed, killing the officer and four men with five rounds.

Captain J. K. Jacosta was killed and Captain R. G. Burch wounded, but the fight continued until well into the morning of the next day, the 19th, when the enemy completed their mopping-up. A few of the Hughesiliers managed to get away; Major Paterson with the others surrendered when the ammunition was exhausted and further resistance impossible.

The Fight at Quarry Gap

When the Hughesiliers and details of the Middlesex and Rajputs were still holding out on the North Shore, Tanaka's second battalion and all three of Shoji's battalions were advancing against our second line.

To meet this attack we had two companies of the HKVDC between Blue Pool Road and Mount Parker. On the left was No 3 Company (Major Stewart), spread out over a wide area. No 7 Platoon (Captain L. B. Holmes) occupied three forward posts on the Ride north of Jardine's Look-out. Lieut B. C. Field with Sgt G. J. White and 18 men of No 9 Platoon occupied the two pillboxes on the south-eastern slope; the remainder of that platoon and No.8 Platoon (Lieut D. J. N. Anderson) held section posts on Blue Pool Road, Stubbs Road, Wongneichong Gap, south end of the Ride and Stanley Gap.

On the right of No 3 Company was the whole of the Mount Butler feature undefended. Beyond that was No 1 Company with HQ in Taitam Valley Bungalow. No 1 Platoon (2/Lieut B. S. Carter) was in Quarry Gap, No 2 Platoon (Lieut J. Redman) at Repulse Bay View, too far away to be of any immediate assistance, and No 3 Platoon, under 2/Lieut R. S. Edwards, with the four carriers, was patrolling the Reservoir Road. On the right of No 1 Company was 'C' Company Royal Rifles, who were holding the eastern slope of Mount Parker, with one platoon near Boa Vista.

This latter company was in danger of having its flank turned by the enemy advance to Sai Wan Hill. The Japanese announced their capture of the hill by a loud-speaker; the position was promptly shelled and a counter-attack was made by two platoons of Royal Rifles, while a platoon of No 2 Company HKVDC was brought up from Pottinger Gap. The counter-attack failed; there was some confused fighting in and around Sai Wan, both sides feeling for each other in the dark. Further west the RA personnel from the battery at Lyemun, which had been overrun, were assisting the gunners of the other 6 inch Howitzer Battery, below Mount Parker, to keep the enemy from overrunning that also. At one point, where the Japanese actually reached the gun position, a gunner officer staged a one-man counter-attack and drove off the enemy single-handed.

Captain Penn, OC, No 1 Company HKVDC received word of the enemy landing at 2234 hours and, as telephone communication with Quarry Gap had been interrupted by shell-fire, went there himself. He informed the Royal Rifles Company of his intention and was told that the platoon at Boa Vista would be sent to the Gap as a reinforcement. Unfortunately the Canadians were unable to find the way in the intense darkness, and by the time they contacted the guide sent by Captain Penn, the fight in the Gap was over.

Captain Penn ordered up the LG section, under Sgt F. L. Curtis, from Company HK Reserve, and sent it to occupy the knoll on the eastern slope of Mount Butler. Cpl F. M. Thompson with six men manned the weapon-pits near PB 45 further down the slope towards Taikoo, and the remaining fifteen men were spread across the gap itself, the Vickers Guns, under Sgt J. P. Murphy, on the right; the LMG's about 25 yards forward on the Taikoo path. In all there were two officers and 29 men. This would have been a scanty force to hold the Gap in daylight; in pitch darkness, where every circumstance favoured the attacking force, it was little more than a forlorn hope.

In view of the non-arrival of the promised reinforcement from the Canadians, Captain Penn sent back for CSM Edwards to come up from Taitam Bungalow with the HQ party, and also intended to withdraw Cpl Thompson's party from their advanced position, but the attack came too quickly. In the Taikoo valley beneath them a few scattered Rajputs were still resisting - the remains of 'C' Company; others had retired and dispersed over Mount Parker. The enemy, despite the darkness, advanced comparatively rapidly, using the path and adjacent tracks.

By 0030 hours Cpl Thompson's position was attacked. The defenders, badly handicapped by want of Verey flares, fired on fixed lines until the enemy rushed the position. Three men, two of them wounded, arrived back at the Gap, another made his way back over Mount Parker.

Soon after 0100 hours the attack came almost simultaneously on the knoll and the Gap. Sgt Curtis's party had only just reached their position on the knoll and had barely time to get the gun in action before the rush swept on to them, but they inflicted considerable loss on the enemy at point-blank range, and then fought it out with bayonets. There were two survivors.

The enemy advancing up the Taikoo Path were at first believed to be some of the Rajputs retreating. Carter shouted, "Who the Hell are you? Answer or we fire," and the reply was the banzai yell, followed by a charge. The little party swept the path and adjacent hillside with Vickers and LG fire for ten minutes and broke up every attempt of the enemy to rush the position. The darkness, however, enabled the Japanese to crawl in close and throw grenades, and also to infiltrate through the very thin line. Captain Penn was struck on the helmet by a grenade splinter and was temporarily stunned. At about the same time the LMG's were overrun. Carter, left alone on the left side, moved to the other flank and found Sgt Murphy, with only three men of his gun-crews left, trying to withdraw his guns, the enemy being already in his rear. Carter ordered him to put the guns out of action and fall back along the Taitam Path. As the Japanese were now through the Gap, Carter, concerned for the safety of the HKSRA battery in the valley behind, withdrew down Taitam Path with Sgt Murphy's party and two others. Penn, on recovering, collected three more survivors, one of whom he sent back to Company HQ to bring up the CSM's party. The messenger never arrived, and Penn, after waiting for about twenty minutes, during which time he had the satisfaction of shooting a Japanese officer in the very act of sending up the success-signal, realised that the position was irretrievably lost, and withdrew to Taitam Bungalow.

In this fight No1 Platoon had 19 killed, wounded and missing.

Meanwhile Carter had got word to Lieut Bompas, commanding the battery, which at once opened fire on the Gap and adjacent ground.

Tanaka's two battalions made no further movement during the night. At dawn his left or easterly battalion, which had penetrated as far as Sai Wan Hill, began to bring heavy pressure against the two companies of Royal Rifles which were holding a line from Mount Parker to Pottinger Gap, linking up with No 5 Platoon (Scottish) HKVDC. His right battalion moved forward into Taitam Valley.

On arriving back at Taitam Bungalow, Captain Penn and 2/Lieut Carter collected the survivors of No 1 Platoon, the HQ party and a few Rajputs - in all, about thirty men - and disposed them to cover the bungalow and the battery.

At dawn the battery commenced shelling the enemy on the opposite slopes, below Mount Parker. This continued for some hours; the Japanese, evidently unaware how small a force was opposing them, made no attempt to advance against Penn's front, contenting themselves with long-range fire.

The Fight at Jardine's Look-out

The three battalions of Shoji's Rentai, as has been said, were moving towards Jardine's Look-out, mainly using Sir Cecil's Ride. Major Stewart received word of the enemy landing from West Brigade at 2240 hours - nearly two hours after the landing had taken place - and asked for reinforcements. These were supplied from the HQ Company, Winnipeg Grenadiers, under Captain Bowden. Four platoons were sent up and were placed as follows:- Lieut Macarthy's platoon was astride the Ride, immediately below the pill-boxes; Lieut Birkett's platoon was sent to occupy the summit of Jardine's Look Out, but as Birkett found the ascent impossible in the rain and darkness, this move was postponed until daybreak; Lieut French's platoon was in the gap between Jardine's Look-out and Mount Butler, where they could use the broken catchwater as a trench; and Lieut Mitchell's platoon was in Stanley Gap. In all there were some 230 Canadians and Volunteers to hold a large area of broken and difficult ground in face of the three battalions under Shoji's command.

The enemy advance party "bumped" the first of our posts on the Ride just before midnight. This post was held by L/Cpl D. Hung's section, which gave the enemy a very warm reception, on the strength of which, apparently, a report was sent back to Shoji that the whole area was "heavily fortified". After about half-an-hour the main body of the Japanese appeared, and L/Cpl Hung withdrew his section to the next post, known as JLO 2. There was a long and stubborn fight here. The Japanese located the position of these forward defended areas by sending "suicide squads" in front, to make as much noise as possible and draw the fire of the post. At JLO 2 they attempted to cut the wire, but the wire-cutting party was detected and wiped out each time. Eventually the position was taken by the Japanese sending over a constant shower of hand-grenades, under cover of which some of them crawled under the wire. After that the fighting was hand-to-hand. Captain Holmes was killed; Sgt E. Zimmern, wounded, gave the order to withdraw to JLO 3 and was killed while trying to cover his men's withdrawal. L/Cpl E. Hing was killed at about the same time. L/Cpl Hung with a few men retired but, being cut off from Stanley Gap, made his way into Happy Valley.

The third post, JLO 3, was not attacked, the Japanese preferring to by-pass it by going up the hillside. L/Cpl F. R. Zimmern, finding that he could do nothing in that area, withdrew his section to Stanley Gap, where he and his men were a welcome reinforcement.

As soon as it became evident that the Japanese were in considerable strength, another request was made for reinforcements. West Brigade then ordered up 'A' Company Winnipeg Grenadiers, under Major Gresham, from

Deepwater Bay; their positions around Little Hong Kong being taken over by personnel from "Thracian". 'A' Company unfortunately missed the way, crossed Violet Hill and became so "involved in thick undergrowth" that Major Gresham halted and waited for daylight. At dawn the company found itself facing enemy troops, presumably from Doi Butai. Major Gresham was killed and the company annihilated.

Shoji's advance troops, working to time-table, waited for dawn before advancing further. Shoji stated that he sent one battalion round either side of Jardine's Look-out and the third assaulted the summit. This delay did us no good, since the promised reinforcement of 'A' Company Grenadiers did not materialise; and it served the enemy in good stead in one instance. Macarthy, whose platoon straddled the Ride, withdrew to his day positions a quarter of an hour before dawn, and it was just at that time that the Japanese advance troops came along the Ride. Their rubber footwear made no sound and it was impossible to see them in the darkness. Macarthy was thus "by-passed"; at dawn three of his men joined Sgt White's party in Pill-box 2, the remainder withdrew across the small valley to protect the Brigade HQ shelters.

Why the enemy did not attempt to rush the two pill-boxes under cover of darkness remains a mystery. They certainly knew where they were. It was an error that cost them dearly when daylight came.

At about 0630 hours, at first light, the Japanese advance party "bumped" the section post held by L/Cpl R. Ma's section. They did not apparently expect this and there was considerable confusion and shouting, and the main body halted, bunched on the Ride. There was just light enough for Lieut Field to see this enemy concentration in his rear; he opened fire from PB1 and "the Nips caught a packet". Massed on the Ride, they were unable to deploy or take cover quickly. This broke up the first assault on Wongneichong Gap.

L/Cpl Ma's section gave a good account of itself and held the attack for about a quarter of an hour. The leading enemy platoon which had advanced in close formation was almost completely "written-off" and the enemy suffered many more casualties before they eventually worked around the flank and took the position with a bayonet charge. Of the nine men in the section five were killed and three wounded.

Just before 0700 hours a company of Japanese, working up the stream-bed to avoid the fire from the pill-boxes, rushed Wongneichong Gap, driving back Cpl M. S. Lau's section there. The success-signal went up, but the customary shrill yell of triumph was rudely cut short by Field who opened fire on the enemy while massed in the Gap and again scattered them with heavy losses.

Cpl Lau, with three of his men, held the Gap until the enemy took Police-Station Knoll (now occupied by House No 1, Repulse Bay Road). Lau, the last survivor, cut his way through to the Deepwater Bay Road and joined with 'B' Company, Middlesex.

From Wongneichong Gap the Japanese started an attack up the hill towards Stanley Gap, held by Mitchell's platoon of Canadians and two sections of No 3 Company, under Lieut Anderson. The attack made little headway against Anderson's LMG's and Field gave valuable assistance by shooting up parties of the enemy who tried to make their way along the ridge. By 0730 hours, however, another enemy attack developed from the east side, the enemy coming along the slope above Reservoir Path. Mitchell's men had to change front to meet this threat. The Japanese were in overwhelming force and Mitchell's men were literally swamped. A few got away; Mitchell was killed, as were most of his men. Anderson was killed, Stewart was wounded and the position was overrun. Stewart, with six others, retired into the Company HQ shelter; another party, under CQMS E C. Fincher, held out in the store-shelter-until the Japanese blew in the front with a mortar-bomb in the afternoon. Except for these, the Gap was in enemy hands by 0820 hours.

The identity of this force which came from the east and overran Stanley Gap is not clear. It seems most likely that it was the battalion which Shoji declared he sent round the east side of Jardine's Look-out. At his trial, however, he stoutly maintained that none of his troops had attacked Stanley Gap, and that the capture of the position and the subsequent atrocities committed there, were the work of a battalion sent forward by Colonel Doi. As the court exonerated Shoji, the historian must do the same. The atrocities referred to were committed on wounded Canadians and Volunteers after the Gap was overrun. These were mishandled in various ways; one was kicked to death, others finished off with rifle butts and bayonets. The fate of the other wounded, who were left to die slowly of gangrene and thirst, was probably more unpleasant. The further advance of the enemy south of Wongneichong Gap, which was the task of the Doi Butai, was checked by a mixed party of men of the HKRNVR, under Lieut-Commander J. C. M. Grenham and Lieut-Commander P. Dulley[3], and Indian gunners of the HKSRA, under Major Crowe. Before dealing with this phase, it will be well to continue the account of those units which were still resisting in the Jardine's Look-out area.

Macarthy's platoon and two sections of No 3 Company (under Cpl J. F. C. Mackay and L/Cpl G. E. K. Roylance) which were posted west of the Gap, were not overrun. They fell back to guard the shelters at Brigade HQ and Blue Pool Road. Captain Bowden[4], OC, HQ Company Grenadiers, arrived and took command, but was killed a few minutes later. At 1000 hours the Japanese took

---

[3] Lieut-Commander Hugh W M Dulley, HKRNVR
[4] Capt Alan S. Bowman, Winnipeg Grenadiers

Brigade HQ and Brigadier Lawson, the Brigade Major and all personnel of Brigade HQ were killed. Macarthy's men still continued to hold the shelters on the north side of the road and the two Volunteer sections withdrew to the road-bend, to wait for the counter-attack.

In Mount Butler Gap, French's Canadians held out until about 0900 hours, when they were attacked from both sides. French was killed; the survivors tried to cut their way through to Taitam Valley, but very few succeeded.

On the summit of Jardine's Look-out, Birkett's men, coming up soon after dawn, found the Japanese in great strength swarming up the northern slope, they having also apparently found the ascent impossible in darkness. A stubborn fight continued throughout the morning, the Canadians holding on gallantly against very heavy odds -according to Shoji, there was an entire battalion there. Birkett was twice hit and finally killed; his platoon sergeant, Marsh, was wounded and disabled. Eventually at about 1330 hours the survivors made their way down the west side of the hill, hoping to reach Happy Valley. Field went out from PB 1 and rescued a party of five, whom he brought back to his position.

The defence of the pill-boxes was a truly magnificent effort. Field had twenty of his own men with three Canadians, and this small party, completely isolated and unsupported, held the pill-boxes throughout the day, inflicted very heavy losses and occupied the attention of the greater part of Shoji's force. During the day, the Japanese were unable to make use of the Ride or to occupy Wongneichong Gap, the slopes of Mount Nicholson or the ground to the westward down to Tai Hang Road. This would have afforded an excellent line for a counter-attack on Jardine's Look-out, but, as Brigade HQ was in enemy hands, it was impossible to get a message through.

After the enemy took Stanley Gap, efforts were concentrated on the pill-boxes, heavy mortar-fire alternating with infantry attacks and attempts to infiltrate. All attacks were repulsed. The dead ground near the pill-boxes enabled enemy snipers to crawl in close and fire at the loop-holes, and in PB 1 seven out of the crew of eight were hit, but the fire of the machine-guns never slackened. L/Cpl K. C. Hung, badly wounded, carried on pluckily throughout the day, and Pte G. White, at a time when Lieut Field had been wounded for the first time and was lying unconscious, set a fine example by keeping up rapid and accurate fire, though his loop-hole was the most exposed, and three men in quick succession had been hit there. Later he was wounded and the gun wrecked, but he carried on with a rifle.

The enemy made two attempts to advance along the catch water which runs between the two pill-boxes. The first was frustrated by Lieut Field, who went out and lobbed grenades into the catchwater; the second by L/Cpl N. Broadbridge and Ptes G. Jitts and T. Leonard. About midday an attack nearly succeeded, a party of Japanese getting on top of PB 1 and throwing grenades in through the loop-holes. This enemy party was wiped out with the help of some of the men from PB 2. By this time PB 1 was a complete wreck with all guns knocked out. Lieut Field then moved his remaining men into the open and continued the defence with rifle and LMG fire. By 1500 hours the Japanese gave up infantry attacks, contenting themselves with intensified mortar-fire. Field decided to hold the position with a few men only and sent away L/Cpl Broadbridge with a dozen men, including five walking wounded. These got through safely and joined the Middlesex at Leighton Hill.

During the day Lieut Field was severely wounded on four separate occasions, and the wonderful determination and fighting spirit he showed under the circumstances was beyond all praise. At about 1800 hours he collapsed from exhaustion and loss of blood. L/Cpl K. C. Hung had again been wounded-mortally, Cpl Rix (Canadian) was disabled, and of the little party only Sgt White was unwounded. Just before dark, a Japanese officer came in with a flag of truce. Sgt White went out to meet him. The officer offered them their lives if they surrendered, and White, who was down to his last five rounds, accepted the terms.

To do them justice, the Japanese kept their word after their own fashion. The seriously wounded men were left to die; but those able to walk were spared; and those who survived the next day's march lived to reach the prison camp.

In Wongneichong Gap, Major Stewart with CSM V. H. White, Sgt G. Winch and four OR remained in the HQ shelter. The enemy apparently decided that it would prove too expensive to "winkle them out", and made no attack on the shelter. On the night of the 22nd, having been without food for four days and running short of ammunition, they evacuated the position and made their way, in pairs, back to our lines.

Colonel Shoji stated in his war-diary that "after sixteen hours of hard fighting" his troops took their objectives. He gave his losses as "over 800". The defenders lost 160 out of 230 men engaged. Of nine officers, six were killed and two wounded.

The Action of the MTBs

December 19th

Meanwhile a very gallant attempt was being made by the Second Motor Torpedo Boat Flotilla, commanded by Lieut-Commander G. H. Gandy, RN (retired), to attack enemy shallow-draft vessels which were ferrying troops from the mainland to the island. These were presumably the two battalions of the Divisional Reserve; the two Divisional Artillery Groups and other units.

At 0730 hours on the 19th, six Motor Torpedo Boats made a rendezvous at Green Island and were ordered to attack in pairs. MTB's 07 (Lieut R. W. Ashby, HKRNVR) and 09 (Lieut Kennedy, RNVR), made a successful attack and sank one enemy landing-craft, set another on fire and forced a third to run for the beach. On their return, 07 was hit in the engine-room by a shell and had to be towed back by 09. The second pair then went into the attack, but by this time the Japanese had stopped ferrying across the harbour. MTB 18 (Lieut J. B. Colle, HKRNVR) received a direct hit in the conning-tower, killing the commander and the Lieutenant (Sub-Lieut D. McGill, HKRNVR). Completely out of control and burning heavily, she rushed into the sea-wall alongside Chatham Road near the Kowloon Docks. MTB 11 (Lieut J. C. Collingwood, RN) was hit, but managed to get back.

By now the Japanese were shelling from both sides of the harbour and Japanese aircraft were attacking the MTB's with light bombs and machine-gun fire. Under the circumstances, the other two boats were ordered not to attack, but the signal apparently never reached MTB 26 (Lieut D. W. Wagstaff, HKRNVR), which went into the harbour and was last seen lying stopped off North Point, under heavy fire. Her captain, the Lieutenant (Sub-Lieut J. C. Eager, HKRNVR), the Coxswain (Petty-Officer Bowden) and all hands were killed.

Our casualties in this action were almost 50 per cent of personnel engaged. Two boats were sunk; one badly damaged and one slightly damaged, and it was not thought that adequate results would accrue from any further similar attempts.

For his part in this action Lieut R. W. Ashby was awarded the Distinguished Service Cross.

The Withdrawal from the Shek-O Peninsula and the Evacuation of the Taitam Valley

Within little more than twelve hours from their initial landing, the Japanese had made substantial progress. Shoji's men were engaged in "mopping-up" in the Jardine's Look-out area, which, as we have said, occupied them for most of the day. A battalion of the Doi Butai had taken West Brigade HQ and was pressing southwards from Wongneichong Gap. In the east of the island one of Tanaka's battalions was in Taitam Valley, with nothing to oppose it except one HKSRA battery and Penn's handful; the other battalion was attacking the two companies of Royal Rifles on the east slopes of Mount Parker.

The enemy advance to Sai Wan threatened East Brigade HQ.

This consequently withdrew to Stone Hill near Stanley. Brigadier Wallis also decided to withdraw the troops from the Shek-O Peninsula, which, in the event of an enemy break-through at Sai Wan, would be cut off. These troops comprised two platoons of Royal Rifles and two HKVDC units; the 1st Battery which was at Cape D'Aguilar and No 2 (Scottish) Company which was distributed along the peninsula from Pottinger Gap to Island Bay, with HQ in Mitchell's bungalow.

At 0400 hours No 2 Company was told to hold itself in readiness for a counter-attack, but the order was countermanded; and at 0800 hours orders were given to retire on Stanley. At Cape D'Aguilar Captain Rees destroyed his guns and 1st Battery proceeded by road. Bdr P. Wilson, Acting BQMS, was sent back to obtain supplies but was never seen again; he presumably ran into the enemy. Captain Crozier, commanding 2nd Battery, which was at Bluff Head, mustered all available private cars and sent them out to assist in the withdrawal. Both units arrived at Stanley at about 1500 hours. The gunners, for the next few days, acted as infantry reserves by day and as coast-watchers by night. Major Forsyth with the Scottish Company occupied Sugar-Loaf Hill.

In Taitam Valley the Japanese made no attempt to attack frontally, apparently believing that they had a large force to deal with. Penn, having with great difficulty established telephone contact with East Brigade, asked for reinforcements. He was told to hold his ground as "a counter-attack was being initiated from Wongneichong area which would sweep the enemy out of Taitam Valley." In point of fact, the two companies in that area were at that moment trying desperately to hold their ground against the whole force of Shoji's attack. This is a striking example of the difficulties of the Higher Command due to the break-down of communications, and consequent absence of up-to-date information.

By 0800 hours the men of the Royal Rifles on Mount Parker were finding it difficult to hold their ground; and the 6 inch Howitzer battery below Mount Parker was in danger of being overrun.

As the morning wore on, large numbers of the enemy made their way past Penn's left flank, and the situation both of his small force and of the Battery became precarious. At 1130 hours Lieut Bompas was ordered to put his guns out of action and withdraw to Stanley; and shortly before midday, Captain Penn was also ordered to withdraw the party in Taitam Valley and No 2 Platoon from Repulse Bay View; 2/Lieut Edwards with the Carriers was to remain to cover the withdrawal of the Royal Rifles from Mount Parker. By 1600 hours the withdrawal had been completed; the Royal Rifles of Canada, Nos 1 and 2 Companies and 1st and 2nd Batteries HKVDC were concentrated in the Stanley area. Thus the whole north-eastern part of the island was in enemy hands; this area included Taitam Reservoir.

The Fight at Postbridge

From Wongneichong Gap southwards the attack was carried on by units of Colonel Doi's 228th Regiment, presumably the battalion which had overrun Stanley Gap; and these found their way barred by the defending force at Postbridge, a large house south of the Gap.

The naval contingent had arrived there by chance. During the previous night a report had been sent to Aberdeen that "a house near Wongneichong Gap was signalling to the "enemy" and a naval party of ten men volunteered to investigate and went up from Cornflower Base at Deepwater Bay. The party included two senior officers, Lieut-Commander J. C. M. Grenham and Lieut-Commander P. Dulley. The house indicated proved to be the HQ of a HKSRA battery, commanded by Major Crowe. The party went on to search other houses, and, soon after dawn, was fired on at close range, returned the fire and withdrew to Postbridge. Here Major Crowe and Captain Atkinson collected some of their gunners.

Soon after 0800 hours the Japanese opened heavy fire on the house. Captain Airey[5] (HKSRA) was killed and Mr G. G. Tinson, the owner of the house, who was assisting in the defence, was mortally wounded.

Contact was made with Naval HQ and Lieut-Commander Grenham asked that a company might be sent from Repulse Bay area along the catchwater; thus enfilading the enemy, who appeared to be mainly around the police-station knoll. This promised reinforcement never arrived. A runner was sent back to the Ridge, asking for Vickers guns and ammunition. The guns were sent - unfortunately, still in boxes and thick oil.

At 1030 hours a reinforcement was sent up from Deepwater Bay. This comprised a naval detachment from "Thracian" and another party of the HKRNVR. The officer in charge of the party, not clearly understanding the situation around the Gap, brought his transport too far up the road and came under point-blank fire, rifle and machine-gun, from the knoll. There were a number of casualties. Most of the survivors and some of the wounded later made their way to Postbridge.

Contact was made with a battery, which opened fire on the knoll and demolished the police-station building. A number of Japanese crawled down the slopes below Mount Nicholson, using their groundsheets as camouflage. They were betrayed by the wind, and were severely shot up.

In the early afternoon a party of Winnipeg Grenadiers came up the Deepwater Bay Road, the advance party of 'B' Company which had been sent to

---

[5] Capt Avery

participate in the counter-attack on Wongneichong Gap. This diverted the enemy's attention and there was a lull in the attack on Postbridge.

The Counterattack on Wongneichong Gap and Jardine's Lookout

As has been said, by 1000 hours West Brigade HQ had fallen, though the shelters north of the road were still held by some of Macarthy's men. The fact that the whole Brigade staff, as well as the personnel of HQ East Group Artillery had been killed and that Brigade telephone lines were in enemy hands may have been the reason for the delay in making a counter-attack, but it was probably the paucity of troops available for such an effort. It was impossible to withdraw any of the troops holding the shore line from Causeway Bay round to West Bay, since this would merely invite another enemy landing; and the only troops that could be spared were the Royal Scots, and part of the Punjabis and Grenadiers.

At 1100 hours Lieut-Colonel Kidd moved 'B' and 'C' Companies, Punjabis, to the position east of Leighton Hill, to relieve pressure on the Rajputs. From there the Punjabis pushed towards Tai Hang.

It was not until 1300 hours that our counter-attack developed. The two Punjabi companies were ordered to strike north-eastwards towards the North Point Power Station. 'B' Company Rajputs, which included the survivors of 'D' Company, was to advance eastwards from Leighton Hill. 'A' and 'D' Companies Royal Scots were to attack from Middle Gap and the Filter Beds respectively, with Wongneichong Gap as their objective, and 'B' Company Winnipeg Grenadiers was to advance from Deepwater Bay and attack the Gap from the south side.

The personnel of the Field Company Engineers HKVDC at Tai Hang was formed into an infantry unit under Captain K. S. Robertson and Lieut I. P. Tamworth, and attached to 'D' Company, Royal Scots.

Only eight field guns were available for supporting this advance.

By 1630 hours it became clear that the enemy was in much greater strength than had been anticipated. It had been estimated from visual observation that "the enemy in the Jardine's Look-out area was about one battalion strong." As we now know, the whole of Shoji's Butai was there, together with one battalion of Doi's while both of Tanaka's battalions were by now in Taitam Valley, not far away. This constituted a force which, even allowing for casualties, was larger than our total infantry strength.

'B' Company Punjabis (Major Kumta Prasad) made considerable headway, but the Rajputs were held up. The Royal Scots attacked gamely, advancing along either side of Mount Nicholson. Unfortunately, the line of approach from Tai

Hang Road to the pill-boxes, which Field had been keeping open all day, was not attempted.

It was not until after the pill-boxes had been overrun that 'D' Company Royal Scots fought past the shelters where some Canadians were still holding out and one platoon actually reached Sir Cecil's Ride, but had to fall back immediately in face of vastly superior numbers. The attempt to re-take police-station knoll failed and 'D' Company lost heavily there. Captain Pinkerton was, wounded for the second time (he had previously been hit at Golden Hill); Captain Robertson was badly wounded, as was 2/Lieut A. H. Mackenzie, a former member of the HKVDC, commissioned to the Royal Scots. 'D' Company fell back to Mount Nicholson at 2200 hours and joined the platoon of Winnipeg Grenadiers there. Tamworth joined the Canadians in the shelters where he found Lieut-Colonel Walker, who had been wounded earlier in the day. This party in the shelters held out for one more day, but was then forced to surrender.

On the left, or north, of our line, the two Punjabi companies fell back to a line north-west of Leighton Hill.

Throughout the remainder of the night of December 19/20, the position here remained unchanged. The two Royal Scots companies "dug in" as best they could on the east slope of Mount Nicholson. 'B' and 'C' Companies Royal Scots were brought up on their left; then 'B' Company Rajputs; then the two Punjabi companies. Leighton Hill was held by 'Z' Company, Middlesex; this comprised some thirty-five men withdrawn from the pill-boxes along the west shore, commanded by Captain F. T. Man[6].

December 20th

The Evacuation of Postbridge

Throughout the early hours of the night the Japanese had attacked heavily against the small force holding Postbridge, which, since the failure of the counter-attack, was now isolated. At midnight the enemy opened an intense mortar bombardment, setting fire to the house, the whole front of which was demolished. Lieut-Commander Dulley was killed at this time, Captain Atkinson of the gunners was badly wounded and there were many casualties.

It was decided that the position was no longer tenable. Major Crowe and his men retired first. The naval party made a defensive position in rear of the house; the wounded were lowered down the fifty-foot bank, and the party retired and eventually reached Aberdeen in the early hours of the morning. The defence of Postbridge was a very fine effort. It was unfortunate that all reserves were

---

[6] Capt C Man

engaged in the counter-attack on the north side, so that the small garrison was unsupported.

The Japanese Advance

At dawn the Japanese had their forces disposed as follows: on the eastern side of the island was the Divisional Reserve, two battalions strong, preparing to advance southwards from Taitam Valley and Sai Wan to Stanley; Tanaka's two battalions were in the vicinity of Stanley Gap, preparing to move towards Repulse Bay; one battalion of Colonel Doi's 228th was near Wongneichong Gap, ready to advance on Deepwater Bay, the other battalion was still on the North Shore; Colonel Shoji with 230th (three battalions) was prepared to strike westwards from the Jardine's Look-out area, his final objective, as he says in his diary, being High West.

Of these four enemy thrusts, that of the Doi Butai towards Deepwater Bay was the first to materialise, and here the enemy came up against stiff opposition at the Ridge.

The Fight at the Ridge

On the previous day, after the enemy had taken Wongneichong Gap, orders were given for the evacuation of all ASC stores from Deepwater Bay to the junction of Pokfulam and Island Roads. When this was completed, the ASC personnel was formed into an infantry unit and attached to a "mixed force", under Lieut-Colonel Fredericks[7]. This contingent included most of the HKVDC, ASC unit, under Major F. Flippance, with whom were Captain D. L. Strellett and Captain R. R. Davies.

This unit was first sent to Bennet's Hill in expectation of an enemy thrust in that direction; but as the attack did not materialise, a move was made at midnight, December 19/20, to the Ridge. On their way along the Repulse Bay Road, the party met the wounded naval men coming down from Postbridge. The buildings on the Ridge, five in number, formed the HQ of the RAOC and the troops in occupation comprised RAOC and RASC personnel with a few naval ratings, all under the command of Lieut-Colonel Macpherson (RAOC).

At daylight on the 20th the Ridge came under heavy mortar fire from Wongneichong Gap and there was considerable enemy activity, though no actual infantry attack was made. Later in the day, it was decided to send the RASC men back to Shouson Hill. The advance party, under Captain Strellett, came under heavy fire as soon as they reached the main road, there were several casualties and the party made their way back to the Ridge with difficulty.

---

[7] RASC

During the afternoon the enemy fire was intensified; the enemy snipers were active and at about 1600 hours an attack was launched from the hillside to the east, which was beaten off. The position remained unchanged here during the remainder of the day - the Japanese not pressing the attack but keeping up continuous fire, both mortar and rifle.

The Japanese Advance to Repulse Bay

Colonel Tanaka sent off his advance party before dawn; they moved along the catchwater, which runs along the slope of Violet Hill, and were thus able, unseen and unopposed, to reach a point directly above the Hotel. From this point they attacked. It was 0930 hours when Lieut Grounds (Middlesex) reported that the Repulse Bay Hotel was surrounded and that the Garage was in enemy hands. Grounds had with him a platoon of 'B' Company Middlesex and some naval ratings withdrawn from the mine-control station at Chung Am Kok, also a small party of HKRNVR from Aberdeen. The situation was critical and the only available reinforcements were from the Stanley area.

The Stanley Front

As soon as the situation at Repulse Bay was known, a Relief Force was sent from Stanley. This force had a two-fold task; to break the enemy attack against Repulse Bay Hotel and to attack towards Wongneichong Gap from the south. The attack was led by No 6 Platoon (Scottish Company) under Lieut D. L. Prophet, followed by No 5 Platoon (Lieut W. Stoker) and 'A' Company Royal Rifles, under Major Young.

Prophet's men pushed forward along the Island Road, while Stoker's platoon, working along the flank, engaged the enemy who, in considerable force, were moving down from Violet Hill towards Repulse Bay View.

Contact was made with the small garrison at the Hotel which had been since early morning fighting Tanaka's advance party. The Japanese had occupied the Garage and had with them as prisoners four naval ratings and a Middlesex private. The garage was shelled by a howitzer at Stanley View and a successful attack was launched by No 6 Platoon HKVDC. The enemy suffered heavy casualties and withdrew and the five prisoners escaped.

The Canadians and Volunteers quickly cleared the enemy from the vicinity of the hotel and patrols were then pushed forward towards the Ridge, where Macpherson's force was holding out. A Canadian platoon occupied Eucliff to provide covering-fire for a further advance. This platoon, however, came under heavy fire from the enemy on Middle Spur and suffered losses.

Colonel Tanaka, for some reason, did not press his attack, and matters remained static in this area throughout the afternoon. At nightfall the Canadian and Volunteers held Eucliff, the Hotel and the high ground east of it, while the Japanese held most of Middle Spur and the slopes of Violet Hill. Attempts to push forward and connect with the force holding the Ridge were unavailing.

On the other side of Repulse Bay there was also fighting. Japanese patrols had pushed across the hills and reached Island Road north of Deepwater Bay. This, together with the thrust at Repulse Bay, threatened to cut the island into sectors. In an attempt to clear the route from Aberdeen to Repulse Bay, some of 'A' Company Punjabis were withdrawn from the pill-boxes on the north shore and moved via Aberdeen along Island Road. This party, some forty strong, found the way blocked near Shouson Hill by a strong force of Japanese and throughout the afternoon and night a fight continued here; the Punjabis at first attacking but later, as the enemy strength increased, being forced back on the defensive.

The Northern Sector

West Brigade was now under the command of Colonel H. B. Rose, MC, Commandant HKVDC, in succession to Brigadier Lawson. The command of the HKVDC devolved on Lieut-Colonel E. J. R. Mitchell, OBE.

Throughout the morning the Japanese made efforts to gain the higher ground on Mount Nicholson, held by Royal Scots and Grenadiers. By 1700 hours their efforts were partly successful and they gained a foothold on the main ridge, but the steep ascent to the summit was beyond their efforts. At 1930 hours Lieut-Colonel Sutcliffe launched a counter-attack, sending 'C' Company Grenadiers from Wanchai Gap, via Black's Link. There was artillery support for this, but after half-an-hour's fighting the Canadians were forced to fall back, and during the early part of the night the Japanese made further progress towards the summit. Further north the Royal Scots and 'B' Company Rajputs held firmly.

The Japanese did very little attacking on this day, and possibly were resting their troops after the strenuous efforts of the previous day.

December 21st

The Ridge

Early in the morning, at about 0300 hours, a platoon of 'A' Company Royal Rifles from Repulse Bay area reached the Ridge and reinforced the troops there. The other platoons of 'A' Company and the two Scottish platoons were held up and soon after dawn a heavy enemy attack forced these to withdraw and the Ridge was again isolated. Throughout the day there was desultory fire on the houses.

After nightfall Lieut-Colonel Macpherson decided to send the RAOC personnel to Repulse Bay. Fredericks was given command. A party was sent out, under CSM Hamlon (RASC) to reconnoitre a route along Middle Spur. This party had a brush with the enemy and retired to "Overbays".

The fate of the men who left the Ridge that night is a story of its own, and a grim one. In the dark it was impossible to keep touch; Japanese patrols were on the alert; few of the men knew the direction. A number were cut off. The remainder approached the hotel, which was by then closely invested by the enemy, and had to run the gauntlet of machine-guns as they made their final dash through the glare of a searchlight. Less than a dozen men got through.

Those who surrendered, having lost their way on the hillside, were taken, together with Hamlon's party, to Eucliff. They were tied up and beaten with rifle-butts. Some hours later the prisoners were taken out to the lawn, roped together in threes, and butchered. Hamlon, shot through the face, was left for dead but contrived to crawl away; he was the only survivor.

Many days later Lieut Colonel Ride (HKVDC) saw the corpses of these Canadian and British soldiers piled in heaps, their hands still tied behind their backs.

The force left to hold the Ridge comprised some twenty Canadians and forty of the RASC, half of these from the HKVDC. Rations were short and there was practically no drinking water.

Repulse Bay Area

Major Young[8] launched an attack northwards soon after midnight, under orders from Major Templar, RA, who had taken over command in the Repulse Bay area. The attack went well for a time and made considerable headway. A platoon of 'A' Company reached the Ridge, as has been said. Soon afterwards, however, there was a counter-attack and the Canadians and the Scottish platoons were forced back towards the Hotel. Eucliff was evacuated, being too exposed to enemy fire, and the Canadians were concentrated around the Hotel, the two Scottish platoons occupying the high ground, where Repulse Bay Mansions now stand. Major Templar reported that any attempt to "break through to Wongneichong Gap", with the force at his disposal, was out of the question.

The Battle of Red Hill

In the Stanley sector efforts made during the previous night by 'B' Company Royal Rifles to move northwards by way of Stanley Mound and Violet

---

[8] Royal Rifles

Hill had proved abortive. It was decided to try to link up with the troops in the northern sector by attacking through Taitam Valley, the area which we had tamely given up two days earlier. Brigadier Wallis planned an attack along the main Island Road to Taitam cross-roads, which was to be the first objective. From there, if things went well, the attack would continue through the valley to Stanley Gap. The troops detailed for this operation were two companies of Royal Rifles and No 1 Company HKVDC, all under the command of Lieut-Colonel Home (Royal Rifles).

Captain Penn, with better knowledge of the terrain, suggested that Notting Hill and Bridge Hill should first be occupied, since this would cover the left flank of the road advance, and also fire could be brought to bear from the summit directly on to the cross-roads. It was then decided that 2/Lieut Carter, who knew the country well, should lead the way up the hills with ten riflemen from No 1 Company HKVDC, followed by a platoon of Canadians. The road attack was to be led by the Carriers (No 3 Platoon) followed by the rest of No 1 Company and the HQ Company of the Royal Rifles, under Major Macauley, MC.

The flank party, strengthened by the inclusion of Lieut E. M. Bryden and a section of Vickers guns from No 2 Company HKVDC, moved off at 0915 hours; the road party a few minutes later. Near "Brinville" the Carriers came under heavy fire; one man was killed and F/O Thomson, who was acting as Intelligence Officer, was badly wounded. A section of Royal Rifles, led by Lieut Fry, and accompanied by Lieut Bompas (HKSRA) was sent to occupy Red Hill. Captain Penn took his LMG's forward to where he could bring fire to bear on Cash's Bungalow, from which the enemy was quickly driven.

The Japanese on Red Hill were reinforced, as could be seen from the flanking party. Both Fry and Bompas were killed, and the Canadians were driven back down the slope. The LMG's at the foot of the hill then came under heavy fire, and within a few minutes Captain Penn and 2/Lieut Redman were both wounded and disabled, and Sgt N. L. White was mortally wounded, as well as other casualties. Major Macauley then sent back for reinforcements since it was impossible to advance further while the Japanese held Red Hill in force.

Meanwhile 2/Lieut Edwards with the carriers, followed by some of No 1 Company and a few Canadians, had pushed forward to within striking distance of the cross-roads. An enemy battery on the slope beyond the reservoir was engaged by the Carriers and most of the gunners were shot down. Edwards went forward with the riflemen, covered by the carriers, but found the enemy in strength. Edwards and Cpl J. M. Houghton were killed. The remainder fell back to the carriers, where Sgt G. Lemay took charge. Lemay decided to stand his ground, hoping that the flanking party would soon afford covering-fire for another attack on the enemy position.

Carter and his ten men took the crest of Notting Hill without difficulty, but Bridge Hill was strongly held. Captain Clark, with a platoon of Canadians, came up, and an obstinate fight continued for several hours. The Japanese were eventually driven off the crest of the hill by the expedient of setting fire to the undergrowth. Bryden then brought up his MG's and, at about 1400 hours, fire was directed on to the cross-roads, but by that time Lemay's small party, outnumbered and outflanked, had fallen back. Fire was then directed, at extreme range, on to the crest of Red Hill, but with little apparent effect. At about 1600 hours enemy light tanks were seen on the road near Taitam Tuk Dam, and these were engaged by Bryden's guns.

By 1700 hours the Japanese on Red Hill had been reinforced, and now outnumbered the attackers heavily. Major Macauley ordered his troops to fall back to the vicinity of Palm Villa. At 1800 hours the flanking party was recalled - and that ended the fight for Red Hill.

Sgt Lemay's party had only just returned, when orders came that they were to proceed to Repulse Bay Hotel to assist in the defence there. There were only two carriers left. Sgt Lemay's party set off at 1800 hours, reached the hotel without incident, and took an active part in the defence there, as will be told later.

Deepwater Bay and Shouson Hill

Colonel Doi's forces had already isolated the Ridge and pushed on across the golf-course. By 0600 hours they were attacking Pill Box 14 and Brick Hill, both held by men of 'A' Company Middlesex. HMS Cicala (gunboat) was sent round from Aberdeen. The gunboat entered Deepwater Bay and vigorously shelled the enemy, breaking up the attack for a time. The Japanese aircraft attacked her with bombs and machine-gun fire, and she was eventually holed and sank later in Lamma Channel.

Throughout the previous night, as has been said, forty men of 'A' Company Punjabis had been engaged with the enemy at Shouson Hill. They had fought hard and had lost nearly half their strength. Lieut-Colonel Kidd went to the scene himself. He was killed and only four of the Punjabis were left standing.

Captain (temporary Major) A. J. Dewar (RASC) with some twenty of the HKRNVR occupied and held the two houses on top of Shouson Hill. This "island of resistance" fought magnificently and held out until the final surrender four days later. Major M. Hanlon[9] (RAOC), with a few of his men, held the RAOC Depot at Little Hong Kong while Major H. Marsh (Middlesex) collected some fifty men, of various units, and defended the "Combined Company HQ" in the same area.

---

[9] Lieut M C Hanlon, RAOC

These individual efforts prevented the Japanese from penetrating further but PB 14 was taken and the Middlesex position on Brick Hill was overrun, despite gallant resistance. Some days later (on the 29th December) Lieut-Colonel Ride saw on the beach a pile of headless corpses, with hands and feet tied, which showed what had been the fate of the wounded men of the Middlesex.

At the seaward extremity of Brick Hill there was the 17th Battery HKSRA. The OC Captain Bartram, went out in front of the position with a tommy-gun and a bucket of grenades, and put up a stout fight before being killed. Lieut Fairclough[10] conducted the defence from the gun position. The position was eventually overrun. Fairclough was wounded and left for dead. Under cover of darkness he climbed down the cliff to a cave, where he remained for four days. He then swam to Aberdeen, only to find that the fighting was over. He later escaped from Shamshuipo Camp - but that is another story.

The Northern Sector

In this area the Japanese at dawn pushed forward vigorously at Mount Nicholson and along Black's Link, forcing back the Royal Scots. They also pushed back our line further north, which exposed the flank of 'B' Company Punjabis, which had been moved across to fill the gap between the Royal Scots and the Rajputs. Major Prasad withdrew his company to conform.

At 0700 hours Brigadier Rose arranged another counter-attack, and 'C' Company, Winnipeg Grenadiers attacked from Middle Gap. Some ground was made but the Japanese were firmly dug in on the eastern slope of Mount Nicholson. At 0815 hours the Canadians fell back; the enemy attacked in turn, and finally by about 1000 hours reached the crest of the hill. From this position they could command the whole of the western slope, Middle Gap and the east slope of Mount Cameron. The Grenadiers on Black's Link had to withdraw, and our next "strong point" was Mount Cameron, held by 'C' Company Grenadiers.

As a reserve for this area, men of 'D' Company Punjabis were withdrawn from the pill-boxes on the north shore and sent to Wanchai Gap, at which place were now located the HQ of both West Brigade and the Grenadiers.

The Japanese followed up their success at Mount Nicholson by making an attack along King's Road, while from a position near the Power Station they directed a heavy mortar fire on to the Naval Yard. At 1030 hours there was another enemy landing, this time in the Causeway Bay area; and it was reported that the "house-tops in the area were crowded with them". This force was presumably the advance party of either the Suzukawa or the Kanki Butai, both of which were brought across during this and the following day. An AA Lewis-gun

---

[10] RA

post at Watson's Factory, Causeway Bay, manned by men of No 6 Company HKVDC, was overrun. By noon the Japanese were pressing their attack down King's Road, and every gun in the Naval Yard was out of action, due to intensive mortar fire.

Our "Line" now ran as follows:- West side of Causeway Bay Leighton Hill - Wongneichong Village-Mount Cameron-Bennet's Hill. The units holding it were, from North to South, 'C' Company Punjabis; 'Z' Company Middlesex; 'B' Company Rajputs; 'B' Company Punjabis; four companies of Royal Scots; 'C' Company Grenadiers (on Mount Cameron); 'D' and 'B' Companies Grenadiers, holding from Mount Cameron to Bennet's Hill, inclusive; then mixed units of 'A' Company Middlesex, Sappers, Naval Ratings, Officers and men of the. HKRNVR and men of administrative details.

At Repulse Bay there were 'A' Company Royal Rifles (less one platoon); a platoon of Middlesex; a naval party; two platoons of No 2 Company HKVDC and the Carriers from No 1 Company HKVDC.

At Stanley there were - the remainder of the Royal Rifles, 'C' and part of 'D' companies Middlesex, withdrawn from the pill-boxes; 1st and 2nd Batteries HKVDC and the residue of 1 and 2 Companies HKVDC.

Of the other HKVDC units, No 3 Company, having lost all its officers and 70 per cent of its personnel, had practically ceased to exist. Some of its survivors were with the Middlesex at Leighton Hill, some at Stanley, some attached to No 6 Company HKVDC. Nos 4 and 7 Companies, which were much below strength, were forming a second line of defence behind Mount Cameron. No 5 Company was in the Mount Davis area, in case of a surprise landing in the West Point area. No 6 Company was still distributed along the North Shore on AA defence. 3rd Battery was still on Aberdeen Island. 4th and 5th Batteries had been "written-off". The Armoured Car Platoon, with only two vehicles left, was operating in the North Sector. It had done excellent service during the two counter-attacks at Wongneichong Gap.

December 22nd

The Last Fight at the Ridge

Early, at about 0500 hours, a telephone message was received from Repulse Bay that all officers and men capable of doing so should retire after dark and make for the hotel. At 1000 hours the Japanese made an attack, which was beaten off with considerable loss to the enemy, but it was evident that this was only the prelude to a full-scale assault on the Ridge. Fortress HQ left the decision to Macpherson, as to whether to fight it out, try to withdraw or surrender.

Both food and water had run out by now. At 1500 hours the Japanese opened with shell and mortar fire and it was clearly only a question of time before the houses were completely demolished. Lieut-Colonel Macpherson then ordered Captain Strellett to put out a white flag. The latter did so, and had it shot out of his hand by a machine-gun burst. Lieut-Colonel Macpherson then walked to the door holding a flag, and fell, badly wounded. This ended the attempt to surrender.

Orders were then given for the evacuation of the position that night. Two men remained to take care of the wounded. The forty officers and men who were left split up into small parties and made their way over the hills. They had barely gone before the Japanese broke in. They found only Lieut-Colonel Macpherson and about thirty other wounded. These were treated in the same manner as the prisoners at Eucliff. Six days later Lieut-Colonel Ride saw their corpses piled in a heap some fifty yards from the house.

Captain Strellett's party reached "Twinbrooks", where, on the morning of the 24th, they were surrounded and had to surrender.

Another party, with CSM S. D. Begg in charge, made for Repulse Bay, which was already in enemy hands. At Eucliff they were fired on, went over the wall and took refuge in a natural cave below the house, where they found several Canadians. The following night (the 23rd) Begg gave orders that all who could swim were to follow him and at 1930 hours he led the way into the water. At that moment CSM Hamlon "a mess of blood" joined the party having just left the scene of the Eucliff massacre.

The phosphorescence in the water betrayed the swimmers and the Japanese swept the surface of the bay with machine-gun fire. Some of the swimmers were hit; some died later of cold and exhaustion in the water. It was not until 1700 hours on the 24th that Begg and two others reached Stanley, after nearly twenty-two hours in the water. CSM Hamlon remained, and later joined a party, including Major Young and CQMS J. Meyer (HKVDC) which reached Lamma Island.

Withdrawal from Repulse Bay

During the previous night the men of the Royal Rifles had made a great effort to push forward to Altamira on the main road and so cover the withdrawal from the Ridge; but they were pushed back by overwhelmingly superior numbers and by dawn were back in the hotel area. Throughout the morning Repulse Bay was under heavy mortar fire from the enemy on Middle Spur. Sgt Lemay took his Carriers into action against them and Lieut Prophet moved No 6 Platoon to the ridge immediately south-west of the hotel and) engaged the enemy with MG and LMG fire. With the assistance of the artillery in the Stanley area the position was partially stabilised. The Japanese, however, continued their attacks fiercely. Their two battalions, though much reduced in numbers, were numerically far superior to the defending force. One of the Carriers received a direct a hit near the entrance to the hotel and the other was later put out of action near South Bay Road Bridge. Sgt Lemay's party was then attached to No 6 Platoon. The Canadians were forced to fall back to the hotel, leaving the Volunteers holding the ridge above.

Major Templar decided that the position was no longer tenable. Defence of the hotel itself with the enemy holding all the higher ground, would be impossible. He gave orders for a withdrawal under cover of night. The position was complicated by the presence of civilians, including women and children. It was first decided that they should accompany the troops and No 6 Platoon was detailed to act as guard for these civilian evacuees. The order was cancelled later as, it was decided that the civilians would run far greater risk by making their way through enemy patrols than by remaining in the hotel.

The evacuation was to be made via the tunnel leading from the hotel to the Lower Beach Road and thence past the Lido up to the main Island Road; from there the withdrawal would be either by the road or over Stanley Mound. To safeguard this route it was essential that the bridge crossing the Lido Road should be occupied and held to prevent the enemy coming from the direction of Repulse Bay View towards Lower Beach Road. No 6 Platoon was detailed for this task and Lieut Prophet moved with his platoon towards Violet Hill area and throughout the afternoon they were in action against the enemy in that area. Several patrols of the enemy were engaged and driven off. In a further attempt to clear out the enemy snipers, the undergrowth was fired. At 1600 hours the platoon withdrew, leaving a section under Sgt T. Stainton, to deal with any further enemy movement in that area.

At 1930 hours the platoon moved out again as a fighting patrol, with orders to hold the bridge at all costs from 2000 hours until 0300 hours on the following morning (the 23rd), by which time it was hoped that the members of the garrison would be well on their way to Stanley. Japanese snipers near the bridge were dealt with, and the Volunteers occupied the bridge without further incident.

The evacuation of the hotel, even when unhampered by civilians, was no easy task. The outposts were withdrawn and the men assembled in the hotel, but the Japanese pressed forward the moment the outposts moved in. An enemy patrol entered the north wing of the hotel, but these intruders were detected and dealt with quietly and unobtrusively. Lieut "Benny" Proulx (HKRNVR) was detailed to lead the party, as having most knowledge of the country. The troops were all in their stocking-feet to avoid noise, but the first three men who went down the narrow tunnel made such a din, their steel helmets and accoutrements rattling against the sides, that Major Templar decided to risk sending the remainder out by the road. Proulx, missing the others, returned up the tunnel to the hotel, but found only Japanese officers to whom to report, so made a hasty exit. The men followed the route indicated as far as the main Island Road, then split into small parties and made their way by devious routes over the hills. All reached Stanley safely, though one party of three, whose sense of direction is evidently not their best asset, found themselves at dawn back at the hotel, with all the weary work to do again.

Most of the wounded were removed with the troops, but two Scottish Volunteers had to be left behind, and these owe their lives to the hotel nursing sister, who on numerous occasions stood between them and the Japanese bayonets during the next three days.

Meanwhile No 6 Platoon was covering the retirement by holding on to the bridge. Right well did they perform their task. At 2000 hours, just before the evacuation started, the Japanese made a fierce attack on the bridge. They overran Cpl Sharp's section, but were driven off by a bayonet charge and later by LA fire. Intermittent assaults were made during the next five hours, but all were repulsed; and the Volunteers, having held their position for the stipulated time, withdrew at 0300 hours on the 23rd. They went back along the main road. Near Frederick's house they encountered a party of Japanese whom they put to flight with hand-grenades and a tommy-gun burst. On arriving back at Stanley, No 6 Platoon joined Nos 5 and 4 Platoons near Stanley View, while Lemay took his party on and rejoined the remains of No 1 Company (now under 2/Lieut Carter) on the isthmus.

The North Shore

In the early hours of the morning Japanese landing-craft were seen near the Naval Yard. The pill-boxes opened fire and the boats sheered off westwards. A report came that an enemy landing had been made. Strong police patrols were sent out through the Central and Eastern Districts and found that the rumour was incorrect.

Throughout the night and continuing up to dawn, enemy launches and landing-craft kept the North Shore defences on the alert. Our pill-boxes frequently opened fire on Japanese craft. There were, however, no surprise landings; and it appears that these demonstrations were intended to compel us to keep troops along the North and East shores.

At Causeway Bay and North Point, however, the Japanese had been busy ferrying more troops across, and had, according to their reports, two more complete infantry regiments, or six battalions, on the island.

The Enemy Battle – Line on the 22nd

The Japanese forces were approximately as follows:- On the front from Causeway Bay to Bennet's Hill they had the remains of the 228th (Colonel Doi) and 230th (Colonel Shoji) Regiments, together with another newly landed Regiment (number not given). Tanaka 's two battalions of the 229th were engaged at Bennet's Hill and Repulse Bay. In the Stanley area there was the Divisional Reserve together with another Regiment, probably under Colonel Suzukawa. They had, in other words, fifteen battalions on the island, though several of these must have been less than half strength. In addition they had apparently five or six battalions of "garrison" troops.

Demolition of Oil Installations

During the morning, acting on orders from the War Office, it was determined to destroy the oil installations on the mainland. Artillery fire was brought to bear on the Texaco tanks at Tsun Wan, the Shell tanks at Tai Kok Tsui and the RN tanks about a mile south of the Cosmopolitan Docks. It was impossible, however, to shell the Socony tanks at Laichikok as they were close to the hospital of the women's prison.

The Enemy Advance along the Line of the Gaps

At 0900 hours the Japanese started an attack in the Middle Gap area. The Canadians on Mount Cameron were heavily mortared and dived-bombed. They could make no reply to the dive-bombing except by rifle fire, and the ground was too rocky for them to dig in.

Later there was a heavy bombardment of the Royal Scots positions further north, particularly the flat ground known as Mount Nicholson Camp. By the early afternoon the Japanese were consolidating their positions on the northern lower slopes of Mount Cameron within a hundred yards of the Royal Scots forward defended localities.

During the afternoon Brigadier Rose judged that, from information available, the enemy was concentrating between Little Hong Kong and Mount Cameron, with the intention of attacking north-west towards Wanchai Gap. As a counter-measure, Nos 4 and 7 Companies HKVDC were brought forward to a line running from Wanchai Gap to Mount Kellett. Lieut G. H. Calvert (HKVDC, HQ) collected all available men from Volunteer HQ and brought them down to strengthen the line.

During the afternoon the enemy attacked the centre of our line, and, though the attack was repulsed with considerable loss to the enemy, a serious gap was made between the left flank of the Royal Scots and the right flank of 'B'

Company Punjabis. After dark an attempt was made to re-adjust the line, but the enemy attacked while the move was in progress, the full force of the attack falling on the Punjabis. Major Prasad had only eight men of his company left owing to casualties and dispersal. An enemy break-through was prevented by 'B' Company Rajputs which took the Japanese in flank. The enemy, apparently unaware of their near-success, did not press the attack. 'B' Company Middlesex, withdrawn from coastal defence, was hurriedly sent in to fill the gap.

On the southern sector of our line there was little action during the day. An attack south of Mount Cameron was pushed back by 'D' Company Grenadiers. At Bennet's Hill the enemy was also repulsed.

Stanley Front

After the enemy occupation of Repulse Bay, Stanley was completely isolated. Our troops occupied the line of hills - Chung Am Kok, Stanley Mound, the Twins, Notting Hill and Bridge Hill; but they were in serious straits. The Howitzers were short of ammunition, only 45 rounds left. Food was also running short. Once again, the Navy came to the rescue and the provisioning and, supplying of the Stanley garrison was carried out by motor torpedo-boats from Aberdeen. The water supply to Stanley had been cut off by the Japanese capture of the Taitam Reservoir, and water had to be strictly rationed.

Conditions Deteriorating

In the evening a serious report concerning the water supply was received from the Director of Public Works. No water was coming from Taitam; the Aberdeen supply was out of action for at least three days, and only a trickle was coming from Pokfulam. "The town (of Victoria) is now helpless."

Our troops were now beginning to feel the strain. The three battalions which had fought on the mainland had been on the move for fourteen days with practically no rest. The past three days had been days of continuous fighting without pause for sleep or opportunity to eat. The Japanese with their vast superiority in numbers could, afford to rest their men; we could not. They had the initiative; we were compelled to try to anticipate their attacks. There was a growing feeling among the rank and file that further resistance merely postponed the inevitable and was not worth the waste of life, though among the higher ranks it was well understood that every day, every hour, was of vital importance to the Empire war effort, and that we should fight it out to the bitter end.

December 23rd

Mount Cameron

Soon after midnight the Japanese made a violent attack on Mount Cameron, held by 'C' Company Grenadiers with a few from other units intermixed. The enemy pressed the assault without regarding losses and eventually superior numbers told. The Canadians, outnumbered ten to one, had their line of defence changed to a number of isolated groups fighting independently. Some of the survivors made their way back to Magazine Gap; others continued to resist. Lieut-Colonel F. D. Field (RA) went forward to Wanchai Gap with the only reserves that could be spared-forty men of the Royal Marines under Captain Farrington. These joined the party of Royal Scots in Wanchai Gap, and patrols were sent forward to Mount Cameron. There was a considerable amount of confused fighting in the dark, and conflicting reports came back regarding the situation. At dawn it became clear that the Japanese held the summit of Mount Cameron, while 'A' Company Royal Scots and the Marines were still in position from Wanchai Gap to St Albert's Convent, which was being used as a hospital. The survivors of the Canadian company were at Magazine Gap in support.

This serious loss necessitated the withdrawal of West Brigade HQ to Magazine Gap.

The Defence of Leighton Hill

Further to the north the situation was becoming critical. The Rajputs, much reduced in numbers and short of ammunition, fell back at about 0800 hours, exposing the right flank of 'Z' Company at Leighton Hill. The garrison at Leighton Hill consisted of thirty five men of the Middlesex and the seven survivors of Field's platoon of No 3 Company HKVDC. They had in all six Vickers guns.

This small force had held Leighton Hill against all attacks for two days. The whole surrounding area had been shelled continuously until it was reminiscent of Flanders in 1918. The Japanese had made a number of unsuccessful assaults; but now, after the withdrawal of the Rajputs, the enemy could infiltrate into the streets and houses adjoining the area.

There were no reserves to send in. At Fortress HQ a party of some fifty men was collected-gunners, spare signallers, and some Royal Scots details returned from hospital and this party was hurried down to Happy Valley, where it occupied the Lee Theatre and the houses adjacent. This served to strengthen the line, but Leighton Hill remained isolated. The enemy attacks continued violently and it seemed to be only a question of time before this "strong point" fell into enemy hands.

At midday our line ran from Pill-box 55 on the North Shore to Leighton Hill; thence to Canal Road, St Albert's, Wanchai Gap and Bennet's Hill.

At 1500 hours the Japanese launched an attack across the racecourse. They were repulsed with heavy loss.

Throughout the afternoon both Wanchai Gap and Magazine Gap were heavily bombed. The position of every gap was unenviable; for the nature of the country was such that local defence was bound to be restricted and confined to the gap itself, thus providing an excellent target for the enemy air force, which did not fail to take full advantage of the opportunity.

At 1730 hours the Royal Scots made a local counter-attack and 'A' Company secured a foothold on the western slope of Mount Cameron. This they held throughout the night.

The Withdrawal to the Stanley Isthmus

Stanley Mound changed hands twice during the day. It remained in the hands of the Japanese and a counter-attack by 'B' Company Royal Rifles failed to dislodge them. The attack came also on Stanley View held by No 2 Company HKVDC. No 6 Platoon held positions on the Chung Am Kok side of Stanley View, and the Japanese made an attack on the forward section but, in doing so, exposed themselves to the flanking fire of Pte Walker's section. These men, at a range of barely 150 yards, had easy targets, and the attacking force was virtually annihilated. The attacks were renewed during the afternoon, the brunt falling on L/Cpl Sharp's section on the hill immediately overlooking Island Road. L/Cpl Sharp was killed and there were a number of other casualties. Prophet then withdrew his platoon to join No 7 Platoon (Lieut Bryden) on the ridge running from Stanley View to Chung Am Kok. Here the Company held its own against infantry attacks, but was subjected to harassing fire from the higher ground on Stanley Mound.

Brigadier Wallis decided that, with the force at his disposal, it was not feasible to attempt to hold; the line of hills, and that his troops could put up a better resistance on flatter ground and on a narrower front, where communication would be easier. The company of Royal Rifles had already withdrawn, and orders were sent to Major Forsyth to bring his men back from Stanley View. Brigade HQ was now reconnoitring the area and preparing three defensive lines; the first, north of Stanley Village; the second immediately south of St Stephen's College main buildings and the third running from St Stephen's Preparatory School to Tweed Bay.

The Shortage of Ammunition in the Northern Sector

The Ordnance Depot at Little Hong Kong, though still in our hands, was virtually isolated, owing to the Japanese pressure in the Deepwater Bay area. This was a very serious situation, for there was a grave shortage of ammunition, particularly for guns and mortars, in the Northern Sector.

After dark, eight ammunition lorries were sent out, escorted by an Armoured Car, with 2/Lieut Carruthers in charge. The attempt to get through was successful, and six of the lorries returned safely with their loads. Without these, the troops would have been in even worse straits. Unfortunately it was impossible to obtain hand grenades, which would have been of the greatest use in the street fighting which was developing in the Northern Sector.

December 24th

The Loss of Leighton Hill

At dawn our positions showed little change. 'Z' Company still held Leighton Hill. From there the line ran along the outside of the race-course to Morrison Hill and Mount Parish. The remains of the two Punjabi companies and the composite company of Rajputs, (now reduced to two platoons) held here. South of Mount Parish were the Marines. The houses near the Monument were still held by details of 'B' Company Middlesex, with whom were some of the survivors of No 3 Company HKVDC. The line through St Albert's to Wanchai Gap was held by the Royal Scots. During the night the Japanese had made no further progress on Mount Cameron and, in fact, 'A' Company Royal Scots was now holding the northern as well as the western slopes. South of Wanchai Gap, the Grenadiers held the line down to Bennet's Hill; these were intermingled with contingents of RN, RNVR and HKRNVR. Little Hong Kong was still holding out and the party of HKRNVR, under Major Dewar, still held the summit of Shouson Hill.

The main enemy attack was in the northern sector, where the Japanese sent in all three regiments, though two of these were by this time less than half-strength. Throughout the morning there was intensive shelling of Leighton Hill. At midday there was an infantry attack which was beaten back with heavy losses to the enemy. By the afternoon, however, the position became untenable and Captain Man[11] was ordered to withdraw if he possibly could. At about 1645 hours the withdrawal was made and, despite the fact that the Japanese had infiltrated past both flanks, most of the defenders succeeded in getting away with their guns. They joined the mixed party of gunners and Royal Scots details in the area between the Lee Theatre and Canal Road. Eight of the garrison, who were

---

[11] Capt C Man, Middlesex

holding the further end of Leighton Hill, found their retreat cut off, and stayed to fight it out. This included two members of Cpl Broadbridge's party from No 3 Company HKVDC - Ptes L. A. Fox and H. Wong. Both of these eventually got away. Fox reached Chungking and later fought in Burma.

Morrison Hill

Following their capture of Leighton Hill, the Japanese directed an artillery barrage on to Morrison Hill, held by a platoon of 'B' Company Middlesex. By 1800 hours all the Middlesex machine guns had been knocked out, and the Japanese then commenced pressing infantry attacks. Major R. E. Moody, DAAG, collected a party of military clerks, spare signallers, military police, etc., some thirty men in all, and took them down to strengthen the force at Morrison Hill. It is worthy of note that this party held Morrison Hill until the final surrender.

Fires in the Central District

There was very heavy shelling from both sides of the harbour during the early part of the night. The artillery fire was directed on to the Central District, the Naval Yard and Victoria Barracks. A large fire was started near the China Fleet Club, which seriously impeded forward movement. Later there were other fires in various parts of the town. By midnight the Fire Brigade, worn out with their efforts during the past few days, asked for military assistance which, under the circumstances had to be refused, as there were no men available.

The Breakthrough at Stanley

Throughout the morning the Japanese had been bringing up troops in the Stanley area with the obvious intention of breaking through the defences on the isthmus. Major Forsyth, HKVDC, took charge of the Stanley Village area, as Forward Commander. The three platoons of No 2 Company HKVDC were sent out to re-occupy Chung Am Kok, to prevent enemy penetration there. Stanley Village itself was held by the Company HQ Group of No 2 Company-ten men in all. On the east of the village was the Stanley Platoon, HKVDC, under Lieut Fitzgerald, with a section of Middlesex machine-gunners in support in No 1 Bungalow. On their right was Captain Weedon's company of Middlesex with part of 'A' Company Royal Rifles.

Monastery Hill was held by a platoon of Middlesex and a section of No 1 Company HKVDC (Cpl E. C. Drown). Further back was the Second Line - the low ridge immediately south of St Stephen's College, occupied by the men of 1st Battery HKVDC (Captain Rees). Sgt Murphy, with another section of No 1 Company was in position at the north-east corner of the prison. At the

Preparatory School were the rest of No 1 Company HKVDC and a platoon of Middlesex.

The Japanese evidently intended to force the defences without further delay. They had enormous numerical superiority, for in addition to the two battalions of the Divisional Reserve, they had another full Rentai - some five battalions in all. They also had light tanks.

The Scottish Company while moving out to Chung Am Kok, passed through the right flank of the Japanese attacking force, and Cpl Leith's section was engaged in hand-to-hand fighting and routed the enemy opposed to them, bringing away with them a quantity of Japanese equipment.

Immediately after the area was occupied, the Japanese attacked vigorously, forcing No 6 Platoon to fall back. No 5 Platoon was cut off and isolated. Being unable to make their way to Chung Am Kok, the men of No 5 Platoon fought their way back to the isthmus and joined the third line of defence near the cemetery. During the night the other two Scottish platoons were attacked continuously. Sgt Stainton, who had throughout done magnificent work, was seriously wounded at close range by a wounded Japanese officer, who was in turn dealt with by Cpl W. E. MacFarlane. Despite all attacks, the Scots held their ground throughout the night.

On the isthmus the attack developed at 2050 hours when three enemy tanks came down the road. A light anti-tank gun, positioned on the road, scored two direct hits on the leading tanks, which caught fire; the third tank escaped. A strong infantry attack was then launched, the brunt falling on the left flank at Stanley Village. The handful of Scots held their ground gamely; Major Forsyth was wounded but refused to go back. The Stanley Platoon and the Middlesex machine-gunners also held their position and every attack was beaten back.

At 2230 hours Forsyth was again wounded seriously and was carried into the school house adjoining the police station. The Volunteers were losing men fast and Fitzgerald asked for reinforcements. Soon after midnight the Stanley Platoon fell back to a line with the Middlesex in the Bungalow. The Japanese by this time had control of the beach on the east side (Stanley Bay) and were sweeping the road-fork with machine-gun fire. Both the Middlesex guns were put out of action; of the 28 men of the Stanley Platoon, fourteen had been hit while every man of the Scottish party had been killed or wounded. By 0100 hours on the 25th the position became untenable and Fitzgerald decided to withdraw. The survivors of the Stanley Platoon and section of Middlesex made a hazardous withdrawal along Fort Road, and were joined by five wounded men, the survivors of Forsyth's party. CSM T. Swan, badly wounded, refused to leave his wounded commander, and remained to "fight it out to the finish". Neither he nor Forsyth was ever seen again.

Fitzgerald's men made their way to the Preparatory School, where Major Templar (RA) and Captain Weedon (Middlesex) were forming the third line of defence.

Meanwhile on the right flank the Japanese had broken through along Beach Road soon after 0100 hours. The Middlesex machine guns had continued firing until they were overrun, and the enemy losses must have been very high. The company of Royal Rifles, barely half-strength, fell back along Prison Road. The break through was complete. Monastery Hill was still held by details of Middlesex and Volunteers, but this was now isolated, and the Japanese pressed on past St Stephen's College to our second line. Here they were held up.

Captain West (Middlesex) had placed a platoon of his company in the centre of the ridge, and the men of 1st Battery HKVDC were holding the line from Prison Road to Fort Road. The Battery had been reorganised into four infantry sections. On the extreme right was Sgt Millington's section lining the Prison Road; 2/Lieut H. S. Jones had a section covering the road entrance to the College; on his left were two sections under 2/Lieut H. G. Muir, one in the vicinity of Barton's Bungalow (now Bungalow C), the other one holding the lower slopes at the south end of the football ground.

At approximately 0200 hours on Christmas morning the machine guns opened fire. The first attack of the Japanese was along Prison Road, and Sgt Millington's men were hotly engaged. Then the enemy attacked across the football ground, where the machine guns took heavy toll; and later all along the line. The attack was heaviest on the right and Millington's section suffered worse. Throughout the early hours the struggle continued along the ridge. Captain Rees was badly wounded and disabled, and the line grew thin as more men were hit. Just before dawn the Japanese stormed the ridge at a point immediately south of the tennis courts. Two of the Middlesex guns were overrun and the enemy broke through the centre of our line. The two sections on the right were forced back towards the prison and Sgt Millington was killed. 2/Lieut Jones rallied his section and brought them back in a gallant effort to retake the position, but the odds were far too heavy. Jones was killed, as were half his men and the rest fell back, still fighting, towards our third line.

The two sections on the left were also forced back. On the extreme left our men fell back to the Preparatory School, where the Japanese were again held up by the mixed force of Middlesex and Volunteers there.

2/Lieut Muir with the remainder held on for some time. They made a stubborn stand in and around Barton's Bungalow. All enemy attacks there were repulsed. Eventually the Japanese brought up a flame-thrower and drove back the defenders, but they retook the position after a fierce hand-to-hand fight. It was a fight to the finish; no quarter was given and the battle-crazed Japanese "fleshed their steel" on every recumbent body, alive or dead. There were no survivors of this section.

This fight at the ridge in which seventy Volunteer gunners and about thirty men of the Middlesex held up the attack of twenty times their number of Japanese, flushed with victory and "fighting mad", will forever be one of the proudest memories of the HKVDC. Of the 3 officers and 65 men of the Battery, 35 were killed and 5 were wounded; the Middlesex lost 22 out of 29 engaged. But the Japanese counted their casualties by the hundred, piled along the ridge and around the bungalow, for the men of 1st Battery, like their comrades of the Middlesex, "died hard".

December 25th

The Last Stand at Stanley

At daylight on the 25th the two Scottish platoons on Chung Am Kok Peninsula found their positions, practically surrounded by the enemy, who were in considerable strength. The Japanese had infiltrated past both flanks and were now in the Chung Am Kok Fort. It was decided to attempt to recapture the fort and Prophet took forward a fighting patrol of twelve men to attack the enemy on the summit of Chung Am Kok height. The patrol worked up to within fifty yards of the objective, and Pte I. F. Grant actually reached the summit, and was killed there. Further advance, however, was impossible; half the men were hit and the patrol was forced to withdraw. The Scottish position was under constant mortar and machine gun fire and the Japanese were closing in. Prophet then decided, after consultation with Bryden, to evacuate and return if possible to Stanley. Prophet, with Ptes Kempton and Tillery, set out in an effort to locate sampans which might be used after dark. They found it impossible to make their way to any of the beaches and, in fact, were cut off from the others, and made their way back with difficulty. It was then decided to hold the position until nightfall, after which each man should try to make his way to Stanley as best he could. Throughout the afternoon the position remained static, the enemy putting down heavy mortar concentrations, but not attempting to come to close quarters. After dark the position was evacuated. Prophet and some others swam across, arriving at Stanley about 2100 hours; the others made their way by devious routes back through the enemy lines. The Japanese were probably not on the look-out, for the surrender had already been made, though the men of No 2 Company did not know it.

At dawn on the peninsula the position was obscure. The men of the Volunteers and Middlesex at Monastery Hill had been forced to withdraw and had made their way back successfully to Stanley Fort. The Stanley Platoon had been ordered back to the Fort, where Captain Skipwith[12] detailed them to act as HQ guard for the last stand. HQ Company Royal Rifles had been recalled from their position north-east of the prison and had fought their way through the enemy, with the loss of one-third of their men. The survivors of 1st Battery HKVDC and of No 5 Platoon were also back at the Fort.

At the Preparatory School there were still the remains of 'A' Company Middlesex (now commanded by 2/Lieut King, the only remaining officer) and part of No 1 Company under 2/Lieut Carter. The Japanese had already infiltrated past their right flank and were in the Tweed Bay area. The two subalterns decided to withdraw, which was the only course they could have taken. Cpl Drown's section had already been brought back from its advanced position and Sgt Murphy's section managed to make its way back from the north end of the prison, complete with guns and equipment.

In the vicinity of the Fort a last line of defence had been prepared, and this was now manned by the survivors of the Royal Rifles, Middlesex and Volunteers. Major J. Watson (HKVDC) withdrew all spare gunners from 2nd Battery, formed them into an infantry unit, under Lieut S. J. G. Burt, and brought them down to strengthen the line.

The enemy made no infantry attacks during the day. It seemed probable that the Japanese commander was resting his troops after their previous day's efforts, and was making preparations for the final attack on the following day. There was, however, heavy shell and mortar fire, and air-raids continued throughout the day. At about 1400 hours Captain Crozier observed a large enemy concentration on the heights of Chung Am Kok (these were apparently preparing for an attack on Prophet's and Bryden's men) and 2nd Battery opened fire with good effect. This drew a terrific bombardment from the Japanese counter-batteries; the No 2 gun was knocked out and extensive damage done to the Battery.

The defenders were in a sorry plight. They had few mortars and no mortar bombs. The Middlesex and Volunteer machine guns had all been knocked out. For weapons they were now reduced to their rifles and the one gun at Bluff Head. They were very short of ammunition. For several days they had been on short rations of food and water. They were completely exhausted after so many sleepless days and nights. They had barely enough men left to hold the line; and it was evident that the intensive bombardment, to which they could make no reply, was only the prelude to a full-scale attack.

---

[12] RA

The Hospital at St Stephen's College

The main building of St Stephen's College was being used as an emergency hospital. In the hall there were some 65 patients, with another 30 in the adjoining class-rooms. The Staff comprised Lieut-Colonel G. D. R. Black (HKVDC), Captain Whitney (RAMC), a Sister from the Military Hospital, six VADs, Chinese nurses of St John Ambulance, together with hospital orderlies.

At 0530 hours on Christmas morning, while the fighting was still continuing along the ridge, "about 150 or 200 Japanese broke into the hospital". They started bayoneting the wounded men, driving their bayonets repeatedly through bodies and mattresses. Lieut-Colonel Black and Captain Whitney went forward in an endeavour to stop them. Black tried to bar the doorway to prevent more Japanese entering. He was shot through the head and "bayoneted dozens of times" as he lay on the ground. Whitney was also shot and then bayoneted repeatedly. The massacre continued until 56 of the patients in the hall had been stabbed to death. The others concealed themselves under beds and in dark corners. One of the few survivors was CSM Begg, who had previously been one of the three survivors of the Eucliff adventure.

In the morning the surviving wounded were driven upstairs at the point of the bayonet and, together with the hospital orderlies, confined in one small room. There were in all about forty of them. Throughout the day, at intervals, men were taken out, one by one, and butchered. Two or three of the seriously wounded men died in the room. At 1700 hours a Japanese officer came in and told them that they were very lucky - "Hong Kong has surrendered; if not, all will be killed". After dark all the wounded men who could stand were forced at the point of the bayonet to carry out the bodies of their murdered comrades and the blood-soaked mattresses to a great fire, which had been made from broken school desks.

Still more horrible was the treatment of the women, all of whom were wearing Nurses' uniform and Red Cross arm-bands. They were confined first in a small room upstairs. The four Chinese nurses were raped by Japanese soldiers repeatedly, then taken away, and have not been seen since. Three of the British nurses were also taken away at intervals, and their dead bodies were seen next day. The other four were raped again and again throughout the morning and afternoon. In the evening a Japanese officer told them also that they were lucky that Hong Kong had surrendered; for in another hour they would have been dead.

The four nurses did what they could for the few wounded men who had survived the massacre. Blankets, dressings and drugs had been destroyed or removed by the Japanese. It was not until the morning of the 26th that Lieut Stoker (HKVDC) was able to reach the hospital and take the four nurses away. The wounded were removed later in the day.

The Hospitals at Happy Valley and St Albert's

The Jockey Club at Happy Valley was being used as an emergency hospital. The Japanese arrived there on the evening of the 24th. The nurses were confined in one room, and four of them were taken out and raped. Further measures, which presumably included a massacre of the patients, were prevented by Dr J. A. Selby, who managed to distract the attention of the Japanese officers until they were too drunk to do any harm.

At St Albert's Hospital the Japanese tied up the members of the nursing staff-sisters, nurses and orderlies and trained a machinegun on them. They were diverted, however, by finding one of their own wounded officers in one of the beds and well cared for, and after a couple of hours released the prisoners.

It is strange that the enemy should have been so pleased at this, since their treatment of our own wounded was either to leave them to die slowly or to "flesh their steel" on non-vital parts. An officer of the Middlesex, shot in the leg, whilst lying on the ground, received two sword-slashes and no less than fourteen bayonet-stabs. Yet he managed to crawl away after dark, and, so far as is known, is alive and well today.

There was only one known case of the enemy picking up a wounded British soldier. Pte J. E. Mogra, of No 3 Company, HKVDC who had been shot through the body, called out in Japanese for water. A Japanese officer came to him and, on learning that Mogra had been born and had lived most of his life in Japan, not only gave him water but ordered that he should be picked up with the Japanese wounded. He refused, however, Mogra's request that the other British wounded should be given water. Mogra died two days later, but told his story to some of the other prisoners first.

The Loss of Bennet's Hill

In the Aberdeen sector the Japanese attacked soon after midnight, and a number of them reached the northern slopes of Bennet's Hill and dug in there. By 0300 hours the enemy again advanced in this area, trying to infiltrate west of Bennet's Hill, where they were held up by the HKRNVR. Desultory fighting continued for some hours. At about 0800 hours the enemy drove in our defences east of Bennet's Hill and made a deep salient. 'B' Company Grenadiers was preparing for a counter-attack on this salient, but the impromptu "truce" which was ordered at 0900 hours prevented this from being carried out. When the period of the truce ended, the opportunity had been lost; for the enemy there had been heavily reinforced. Colonel Tanaka sent in all that was left of his 229th Regiment. By 1400 hours the enemy had completely surrounded Bennet's Hill, and an hour later the men of the Grenadiers there were forced to surrender. 'B' Company Grenadiers, the HKRNVR and the mixed force on the sea-front were forced to withdraw to conform, and it appeared to be only a matter of hours before the Japanese broke through to Aberdeen.

The Last Stand in the Northern Sector

At dawn on the 25th our positions were roughly as follows:- From the sea-front to the Lee Theatre were remains of 'B' and 'C' Companies Punjabis, together with a mixed force of gunners, British and Indian, and Royal Scots hospital cases. Morrison Hill was held by a platoon of 'B' Company Middlesex and Major Moody's, party of "oddments"; with these were the twenty survivors of Captain Man's 'Z' Company. The houses by the Monument were held by the remainder of 'B' Company Middlesex and a handful of Volunteers. 'B' Company Rajputs was on Mount Parish; to the south of Mount Parish were Farringdon's. Marines, linking up with the Royal Scots who held the line from there to St Albert's and thence to Wanchai Gap.

Although there was still a threat of an enemy landing in the Central District, it was decided to remove all troops from shore defences and 'D' Company Middlesex was sent in to support the Punjabis. The residue of 'A' Company Punjabis was also withdrawn from the pill-boxes and moved to Fortress HQ. This left the whole of the shore-line unguarded except for No 5 Company HKVDC.

The enemy pressure against Morrison Hill was to some extent relieved when at 0600 hours a Bofors AA gun was taken down to Morrison Hill, and, at short range, shelled the enemy out of the Craigengower and Civil Service Clubs.

Nearer to the sea-front, however, the Japanese advanced steadily, infiltrating from house to house. Here we were at a serious disadvantage, since we could not make the use of artillery fire in such a congested area without causing heavy loss of life among the civilian population. The Japanese had no such scruples and put down heavy mortar concentrations, some of them lasting half-an-hour. The Middlesex and Punjabis fought splendidly; but what mortars we had were useless for want of ammunition; we had exhausted our supply of hand-grenades and even SA ammunition was running very short.

By 0630 hours the enemy had made a penetration along the sea-front, threatening to outflank the defenders at the Lee Theatre and Morrison Hill. Lieut-Colonel Stewart, commanding the Middlesex, began preparing a second line of defence; O'Brien Street - Wanchai Market - Mount Parish.

At 0900 hours two British civilians, captured at Repulse Bay Hotel, came across under a flag of truce. They told of the incredible number of guns and troops they had seen on their journey, and emphasised that in their opinion further resistance was useless. Major-General Ito sent a message that he would not initiate further hostilities for three hours. His demand for surrender was refused.

The "truce" was apparently honoured by the Japanese troops in the vicinity, but Japanese planes continued to bomb Stanley, Aberdeen and Mount Gough; their artillery continued to shell the Gaps from the Kowloon side and Tanaka utilised the time to reinforce his line at a threatened place.

At midday the Japanese artillery on the island opened up vigorously and there was strong forward movement of the infantry. A tremendous assault was made on Mount Parish and, though the Japanese lost heavily in the attack, they got to close quarters with the Rajputs there. In a hand-to-hand struggle, one platoon of the Rajputs was cut off; the other was driven back. The loss of Mount Parish opened a way along Kennedy Road to Fortress HQ. Road blocks and anti-tank mines were put out, and the last reserve, a platoon of 'A' Company Punjabis, was moved out along Kennedy Road to prevent further penetration there.

Lieut-Colonel Stewart reported that his men, though fighting well, were being slowly but surely overwhelmed by vastly superior numbers and, at 1400 hours, he ordered the troops to withdraw to the "O'Brien Street Line". This was no easy matter since our men were everywhere in close contact with the enemy. The men, by now utterly exhausted, had to retire as fast as they could run and man the new line before the enemy could take advantage of their withdrawal.

The Loss of Wanchai Gap

Further south, the Japanese planes made numerous dive-bombing attacks on Wanchai Gap and Magazine Gap. At the latter they dropped incendiaries which set the hillside alight. By 0900 hours the men of 'A' Company Royal Scots had lost their foothold on the slopes of Mount Cameron, and were back in Wanchai Gap, which was attacked continuously by dive-bombing planes and by heavy concentrations of mortar fire throughout the morning. At midday an infantry attack was made and was beaten back. Air and Mortar bombing was intensified during the afternoon, and at about 1430 hours the Gap was overrun.

Magazine Gap was the next objective of the enemy. Brigadier Rose reported that it could hold out for two hours at most.

The Surrender

At 1450 hours Captain Man reported "the line is breaking". Lieut-Colonel Stewart suggested forming yet another line from the east end of the Naval Yard to Fortress HQ.

It was felt now that everything possible had been done. "This advance of the enemy along the line of the Gaps, the possession of those Gaps by him, thus giving him an open line of advance to the Central Districts, the fall of Bennet's Hill, the isolation of the force at Stanley, the deployment by the enemy of such superior forces and armament, the exhaustion of our troops after sixteen days of continuous battle, with no reliefs for any individuals, our vulnerability to unlimited air-attack, the impossibility of obtaining more ammunition for the few remaining mobile guns, the serious water famine immediately impending-these were the factors which led to the inevitable conclusion; namely, that further fighting meant the useless slaughter of the remainder of the garrison, risked severe retaliation on the large civilian population and could not alter the final outcome. The enemy drive along the north shore was decisive."

At 1515 hours the capitulation was made.

APPENDIX I

Garrison Strength and Casualties

The strength of the military units forming the garrison was as follows:-

	Officers	Other Ranks
Headquarters, China Command	33	
Headquarters, Royal Artillery	6	
8 Coast Regiment, RA	19	518
12 Coast Regiment, RA	16	387
5 AA Regiment, RA	25	563
1 HK and SRA	14	860
965 Det Bty, RA	3	144
22 Field Company, RE	7	213
40 Field Company, RE	7	220
RE Services	18	54
2 Royal Scots	35	734
1 Middlesex	36	728
Canadian Staff	14	78
Winnipeg Grenadiers	42	869
Royal Rifles of Canada	41	963
5/7 Rajputs	17	875
2/14 Punjabis	15	932
HKVDC (all units)	94	1,665
Royal Signals	7	177
RAOC	15	117
RASC	14	183
RAVC	2	3
RAMC	26	146
RA Dental Corps	4	6
RIASC	-	13
HK Mule Corps	3	250
RAPC	3	25
IMS	5	55

Garrison Strength and Casualties

This gives a total of 541 officers and 10,778 other ranks.

Excluding the HKVDC, there were 447 officers and 9,113 other ranks.

The number of casualties, as given in Lieut General Maltby's final figures were:-

	Killed or Died of wounds	Missing		Wounded	Total
Imperial Officers	74	62	}		
Imperial Other Ranks	595	696		2,300	4,414
Indian Other Ranks	376	311			

It is not possible to give accurately the total of killed and wounded for each individual unit. The heaviest loss fell on the Rajputs, who lost 100% of officers and nearly 65% of men. Next were the Royal Scots and the Royal Rifles of Canada, who lost more than 50%. The other three battalions each lost between 40% and 50%.

The naval casualties were given as follows:-

	Killed		Missing		Wounded		Total	
	Off.	O.R.	Off.	O.R.	Off.	O.R.	Off.	O.R.
Royal Navy	2	45	-	14	-	14	2	73
Royal Marines	-	4	-	-	-	-	-	4
RNR & HKRNVR	12	6	5	4	6	4	23	14
HK Dockyard Defence Corps	-	18	-	9	1	4	1	31

Garrison Strength and Casualties

The Japanese losses were never published in any reliable form. Various statements were made, ranging from the somewhat low figure of 1,996 killed and 6,000 wounded, as given in a Japanese paper published on December 29th, 1941, to the very high figure of 7,000 killed and 20,000 wounded, as given in a Tokyo broadcast a few days later.

Lieut-General Maltby's estimate was 3,000 killed and 9,000 wounded; based on the statement by the Japanese commander that he had 9,000 wounded to care for, and therefore required to turn our wounded out of most of the hospitals. A senior officer of the 230th Regiment told the writer that the Japanese landed on the island a force comprising eighteen battalions of first-line troops, each of which included a number of attached gendarmerie, together with four battalions of "garrison troops", and a considerable amount of artillery - a total of about 30,000 men, of whom "nearly half" became casualties. He instanced the three battalions of the 230th regiment, which landed 3,200 strong, and finished with "less than 800". He reckoned the Japanese losses at 14,000 on the island and about 1,000 on the mainland and during the period preceding the landing. His estimate was 4,500 killed and 11,000 wounded. We may take it that the three infantry regiments of the 38th division were, to all intents and purposes, "written-off", and the other three badly mauled.

Their heaviest losses seem to have been incurred during their attacks at Mount Cameron and at Stanley, on both of which occasions their massed "banzai" charges proved very costly.

The high proportion of killed to wounded in our casualty list is due to the fact that we were mainly withdrawing and had to leave the seriously wounded cases behind; and, as has been said, only on one occasion did the Japanese pick up our wounded.

Hong Kong Volunteer Defence Corps - Strength and Casualties

	Strength		Killed & Missing		Wounded		Total	
Unit	Off.	O.R.	Off.	O.R.	Off.	O.R.	Off	O.R.
Corps HQ & S & T	11	41	1	2			1	2
Corps Artillery HQ	3	2						
1st Battery	3	65	2	33	1	5	3	38
2nd Battery	3	83	1	7		4	1	11
3rd Battery	3	75						
4th Battery	3	94		9	1	11	1	20
5th (AA) Battery	2	65		25		5		30
Field Coy Engineers	12	111		8	4	4	4	12
Corps Signals	2	38		4	1	3	1	7
Armed Car Platoon	1	28		4		4		8
No 1 Company	4	100	1	26	2	19	3	45
No 2 Company	4	94	1	24		25	1	49
No 3 Company	4	110	2	35	2	33	4	68
No 4 Company	4	74		4		3		7
No 5 Company	4	94		2		3		5
No 6 Company	5	91		5		3		8
No 7 Company	3	38		2				2
ASC Unit	7	65		26		7		33
Stanley Platoon	1	28		8		6	14	
Pay Detachment	3	14						
Fortress Signals	2	15		1		1		2
Hughes Group	4	68	1	17	1	12	2	30
Recce Unit	1	7						
Field Ambulance	5	164		3		4		7
Nursing Detachment	3	126		3		1		4
			9	248	12	154	21	402

These figures were first made out by unit commanders during the period in the POW camp and have since been amended several times. The strength of the Nursing Detachment was added in 2005.

Twenty-one members of the HKVDC, non-commissioned officers and men, received commissions in the regular forces either before or during the period of hostilities. Of these eight were killed and one died of wounds.

APPENDIX II

Hong Kong Volunteer Defence Corps - Order of Battle

Commandant	Colonel H. B. Rose, MC
2nd-in-Command	Lt-Col E. J. R. Mitchell, OBE, ED
Adjutant	Captain E. N. Thursby, KSLI
Quartermaster	Lieutenant G. H. Calvert
RSM	WO I F. C. Jones, Surreys
RQMS	WO II A. E. Kew
Armourer	A/S/Sgt W. D. White
OC Corps Artillery	Major J. Watson
2nd-in-Command Corps Artillery	Major N. Garland
OC 1st Battery	Captain G. F. Rees
OC 2nd Battery	Captain D. J. S. Crozier
OC 3rd Battery	Captain C. W. L. Cole
OC 4th Battery	Lieutenant K. M. A. Barnett
OC 5th AA Battery	Captain L. Goldman
OC Field Company Engineers	Lt-Col R. D. Walker, MC
OC Corps Signals	Captain A. N. Braude
OC Armoured Car Platoon	2/Lieutenant M. G. Carruthers
OC No 1 Company (Rifle)	Captain A. H. Penn
OC No 2 Company (MG)	Major H. R. Forsyth
OC No 3 Company (MG)	Major E. G. Stewart
OC No 4 Company (Rifle)	Captain R. K. Valentine
OC No 5 Company (MG)	Captain C. D'Almada e Castro
OC No 6 Company (AA)	Captain H. A. de B. Botelho
OC No 7 Company (Rifle)	Captain J. G. B. Dewar
OC Army Service Corps Company	Major F. Flippance
OC Supply and Transport Section	Major H. G. Williams
OC Field Ambulance	Lt-Col L. T. Ride
OC Pay Detachment	Major C. de S. Robertson, MM
OC Stanley Platoon	Lieutenant C. J. Norman
OC Hughes Group	Major The Hon. J. J. Patterson
OC Fortress Signals	Major J. P. Sherry
OC Reconnaissance Unit	2/Lieutenant E. B. Teesdale
OC Railway Operation Detachment Cadre	Major I. B. Trevor
Commandant, Nursing Detachment	Mrs I. M. S. Braude

APPENDIX III

Maps

Two maps were included with the earlier editions of the Record and are reproduced here as a matter of completeness, but at a reduced scale. These are now replaced by five maps to give the location of all places named in the Record, many of which are no longer known by those names or spelling.

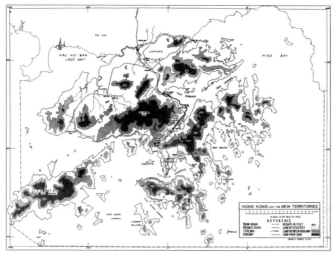

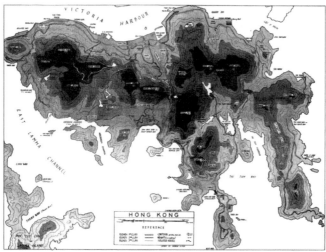

Hong Kong and the New Territories

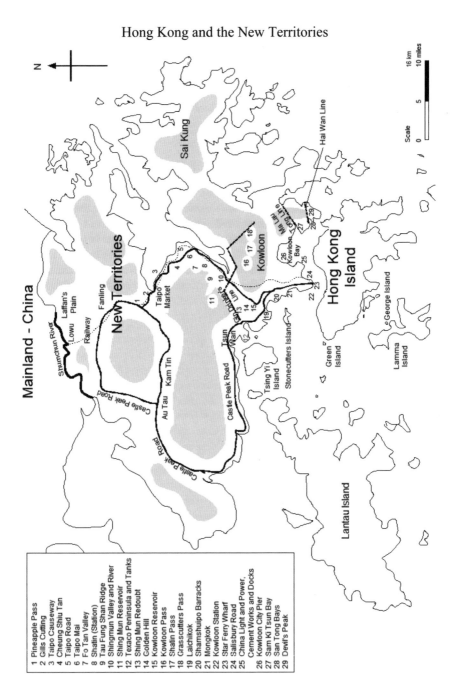

1 Pineapple Pass
2 Gills Cutting
3 Taipo Causeway
4 Cheung Shiu Tan
5 Taipo Road
6 Taipo Mai
7 Fo Tan Valley
8 Shatin (Station)
9 Tau Fung Shan Ridge
10 Shingmun Valley and River
11 Shing Mun Reservoir
12 Texaco Peninsula and Tanks
13 Shing Mun Redoubt
14 Golden Hill
15 Kowloon Reservoir
16 Kowloon Pass
17 Shatin Pass
18 Grasscutters Pass
19 Laichikok
20 Shamshuipo Barracks
21 Mongkok
22 Kowloon Station
23 Star Ferry Wharf
24 Salisbury Road
25 China Light and Power,
   Cement Works and Docks
26 Kowloon City Pier
27 Sam Ki Tsun Bay
28 San Tong Bays
29 Devil's Peak

Kowloon

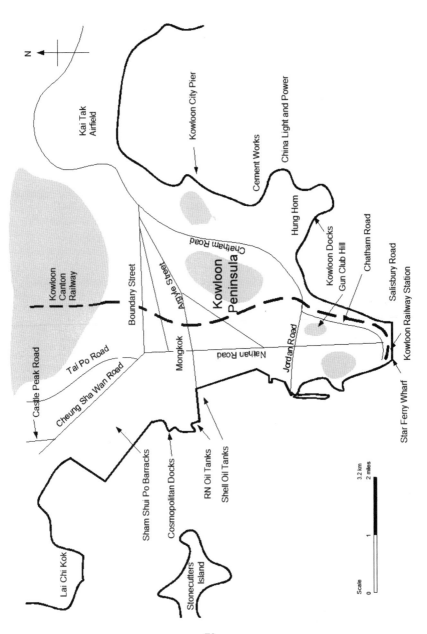

Hong Kong Island

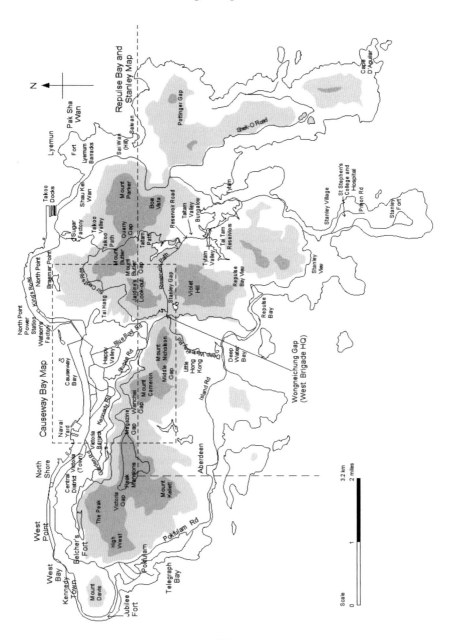

Causeway Bay

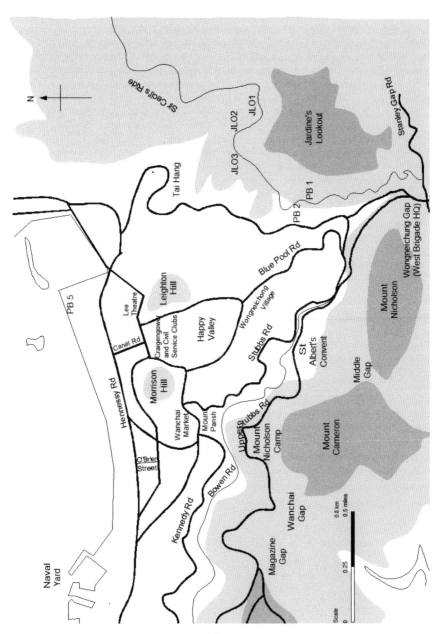

Repulse Bay and Stanley

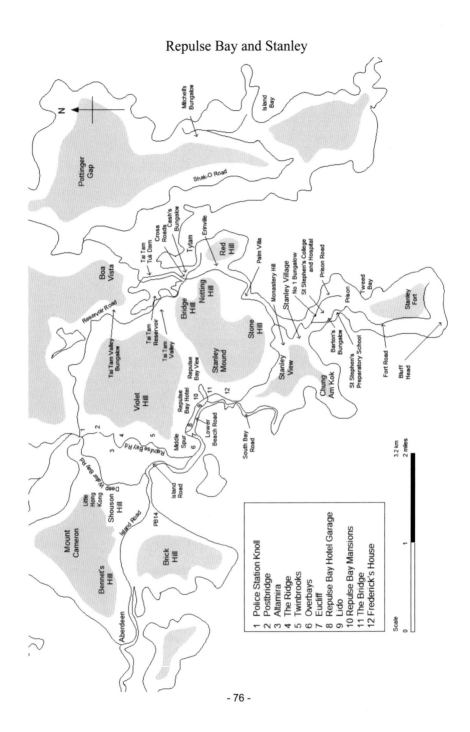

APPENDIX IV

Nominal Roll of the Hongkong Volunteer Defence Corps

In the years shortly after 1945, the Hong Kong Volunteer Defence Corps produced a nominal roll of all those who had mobilised with the Corps during the war. This roll was reproduced in a different format in June 1991, at a time it was known that the Royal Hong Kong Regiment (The Volunteers), the successor unit to the Hong Kong Volunteer Defence Corps would be disbanded. This roll was presented without any further research in the 2004 edition of "A Record of the Actions of the Hongkong Volunteer Defence Corps".

Since that time a correlation has been made with the lists of "Volunteers" prepared by Tony Banham for "Not The Slightest Chance" and Regimental records in respect of those interned in Stanley. Identified errors have been corrected but the list may still include some inconsistencies.

The roll is now presented under the headings of Officers and Volunteers who:
- were POWs at the time of the Japanese Surrender –those who were POWs in Japan at the time of surrender are annotated with "Jpn"
- were interned in the the Stanley Civilian Internment Camp
- were released by the Japanese
- did not enter POW Camps or who escaped in early 1942
- movements after the surrender are uncertain
- were killed in action or died of wounds – includes those who were listed elsewhere as "missing believed killed, presumed dead
- died whilst POW - includes those whose deaths were recorded elsewhere as "unconfirmed" and those who died soon after release from POW Camp
- transferred to other units on outbreak of hostilities
- fought with the HKVDC until the surrender and then joined other units
- did not enter POW Camp and joined the BAAG China Unit and subsequently transferred to join the Chindits in Burma. This list is incomplete but there are no apparent records of all of those who served in Burma.
- did not mobilise
- Nursing Detachment
- HKVDC members who served with the PWD Corps

Nominal Roll of the Hongkong Volunteer Defence Corps

The abbreviations against those who were killed or died are from The Hong Kong War Diary

K - Known grave (At Stanley or Sai Wan military cemeteries)

U - Unknown grave (Commemorated in Hong Kong)

The date after a K or U for those killed in action is the date in December 1941, unless otherwise noted. Dates in brackets are those from the Commonwealth War Graves commission where these conflict with those from "Not the Slightest Chance"

- CCRCC - Cape Collinson Roman Catholic Cemetery
- HKC - Hong Kong Cemetery
- HKJC - Hong Kong Jewish Cemetery
- HKRCC - Hong Kong Roman Catholic Cemetery
- Yokohama – The Yokohama Cemetery, Japan

Prisoners of War at the Time of the Japanese Surrender

No	Rank	Name		No	Rank	Name	
2468	Cpl	Ablong A E Jr	Jpn	3562	Pte	Aquino J L d'	Jpn
2974	Spr	Ablong R S	Jpn	2685	Pte	Arnold G A	
	Lieut	Adam J		4688	Gnr	Arnulphy C	Jpn
4866	Pte	Aitcheson J L	Jpn	3296	L/Bdr	Assesserow W F	
4256	Pte	Aitkenhead G G	Jpn	4165	Gnr	Attwell K J	Jpn
4053	Pte	Alarcon M F		3087	L/Cpl	Azedo A H	Jpn
3712	Pte	Allen C A	Jpn	2324	L/Cpl	Azedo C M D	Jpn
2705	Gnr	Allen D G G	Jpn	3705	Spr	Bainbridge W B J	Jpn
3689	Pte	Allan L D	Jpn	2194	Pte	Baker E F S	Jpn
2606	Sgt	Allen W E	Jpn	DR 30	Pte	Baker E H	
2225	Sgt	Alltree L	Jpn	5310	Gnr	Baker-Carr D'Arcy	Jpn
4544	Pte	Alves A H			Capt	Balean G T	
3581	Pte	Alves A M		1644	Pte	Baleros B B	
3557	Pte	Alves D C S	Jpn	1221	Pte	Baleros J P	Jpn
5220	Pte	Alves E A R		1143	CQMS	Baptista M A	Jpn
2809	L/Cpl	Alves E V		1186	CSM	Baptista M F de P	Jpn
3582	Pte	Alves J L S			Capt	Bard S M	
	Lieut	Alves J M M		5251	Pte	Barker J W	Jpn
3204	Pte	Ameerali J		4133	L/Cpl	Barkus R L	Jpn
4112	CQMS	Anderson G T		DR 298	Pte	Barnes R J	Jpn
4345	Pte	Anderson J W			Capt	Barnett	
4328	Sgm	Anderson W S	Jpn	3819	Pte	Barretto A C M	Jpn
1690	Dmr	Andrews C F		1774	Cpl	Barretto A O	
	Lieut	Andrews W R N		3369	Pte	Barretto H	

Prisoners of War at the Time of the Japanese Surrender

No	Rank	Name		No	Rank	Name	
2718	L/Cpl	Barretto N C		DR 146	Pte	Brown A J	
	Pte	Barron J F		4525	Pte	Brown A P	
	Lieut	Barrow J		3685	L/Cpl	Brown E F	
4050	Spr	Barton B F	Jpn	5094	Gnr	Brown J N	
2964	Cpl	Basta C P		3866	Sgm	Brown J W M	
2877	L/Cpl	Basto A J de C	Jpn	4283	Pte	Brown P J	Jpn
2680	Sgm	Baxter K M		4637	Sgt	Brown W H	
	Pte	Baynes E N	Jpn	5256	Spr	Browne A W	Jpn
2664	Sgt	Bebbington N J	Jpn	DR 297	Gnr	Bruce H D	Jpn
DR 79	Gnr	Benjamin M			Pte	Bruce J	
2975	Gnr	Benuch L J		2226	CQMS	Brumwell W R	
4621	Pte	Berendeef G A			Capt	Bryden E M	
4353	Gnr	Berg S O		2651	Pte	Buckley J F	Jpn
5260	Gnr	Bertram J M	Jpn	3383	Gnr	Bullock H	
	Pte	Bertram J W		3354	Pte	Burch L R	
4696	Spr	Bhumgars G			Capt	Burch R T	
2355	Sgt	Bilson W T	Jpn		Lieut	Burt S J G	
3658	Cpl	Biriukoff A	Jpn	5036	Gnr	Butler E O	Jpn
DR 45	Sgt	Black C		3306	Cpl	Buttfield A G C	Jpn
4329	Gnr	Blake R H		5166	Gnr	Bux S E	
	Capt	Blaker C		3659	Gnr	Bux S E	
4099	Pte	Bluestone R		4732	Pte	Byrne J B P	Jpn
		Bobbington N I	Jpn	3047	CQMS	Cairns M A	
4764	Spr	Bogoslovsky G A		2842	Sgt	Calman A M	
2734	Bdr	Bonch-Osmolovsky V			Capt	Calvert G H	
3729	Pte	Bond A G	Jpn	4868	Spr	Campell G K	Jpn
3534	L/Cpl	Bond C P	Jpn	3708	Pte	Campos L D R	Jpn
2099	Pte	Bond V C	Jpn	1383	Cpl	Campos R A	
3159	Sgt	Booker N J	Jpn	3160	Bdr	Capell R S	Jpn
4981	Gnr	Bosman A	Jpn	3635	Pte	Carnac P S R	
3783	Pte	Botelho C A		2611	BQMS	Carr T W	
	Capt	Botelho H A de B			Sgt	Carroll A T S	
	Major	Bottomley J H			Lieut	Carruthers M G	
3378	Sgm	Bourne V G			Lieut	Carter B S	
2626	Gnr	Bowen J A R	Jpn	3150	Pte	Carvalho A B	Jpn
	L/Cpl	Bower		2080	RQMS	Casey E P	Jpn
DR 270	CQMS	Bower A		3695	Pte	Castilho T M	Jpn
	Major	Branson V C		3531	Sgt	Castro A E H	
	Capt	Braude A N			Capt	Castro C D'A e	
	Lieut	Brett F		4978	Pte	Castro C D	Jpn
4371	Pte	Brezny L		3558	Pte	Castro F M	
3200	Pte	Britto G M		3559	Pte	Castro G F	
2239	L/Cpl	Broadbridge F A	Jpn	3560	Pte	Castro R A	
2092	Cp1	Broadbridge N	Jpn	5037	Gnr	Cazius U E C	
2690	L/Cpl	Broadbridge R T	Jpn	458	Sgt	Charles R H	
2237	Pte	Broadbridge S A	Jpn	4869	Gnr	Cherrill R I	Jpn

Prisoners of War at the Time of the Japanese Surrender

No	Rank	Name		No	Rank	Name	
	Pte	Cherry R M		DR 107	Gnr	Cunningham W L	
DR 291	L/Cpl	Chidell P D A	Jpn	4497	Gnr	Currie A V	Jpn
4689	Gnr	Christensen J V	Jpn	3637	Pte	D'Almada P E	
DR 69	Cpl	Clark B G	Jpn	4364	Pte	Dabelstein L A	
	Lieut	Clark D H		3802	Sgt	Dalziel J M	Jpn
	Capt	Clark W C			Capt	Dand A A	
DR 87	L/Cpl	Clayson H S	Jpn	2930	Sgt	Darby H R	Jpn
3486	Gnr	Clegg E L	Jpn	3209	Sgt	Davies G G	Jpn
DR 178	Sgt	Clemo A B	Jpn		Capt	Davies R R	
3846	Pte	Clemo E R	Jpn		Lieut	Davis D E	
4264	Pte	Clemo F J D	Jpn	4286	Gnr	Davis S G	Jpn
5191	Gnr	Clibborn E W	Jpn	4289	Sgt	Davis T	Jpn
3837	Bdr	Coates W G R	Jpn	4718	Gnr	Davreaux G M	Jpn
	Major	Cock E		3411	Pte	Day D G	Jpn
	Capt	Cole C W L		3310	Gnr	Deane B O'M	Jpn
4661	Pte	Cole H	Jpn		Pte	Debois J	
4335	Cpl	Coleman T		2508	BSM	Delgado J A	Jpn
2115	L/Cpl	Collaco F J	Jpn	2637	Pte	Demee D E M	Jpn
2586	CSM	Collings W R K			Capt	Dewar J G B	
DR 301	Pte	Collis J R	Jpn	3338	Sgt	Dick J	
2865	L/Cpl	Connolly F	Jpn	4566	Pte	Didsbury H L	Jpn
3301	Pte	Conolly W R	Jpn	1718	Sgt	Dinnen A H	
	Lieut	Cooke S J		4823	Pte	Dixon I G N	Jpn
	Lieut	Cooper H G		3221	L/Cpl	Dodd J	Jpn
	Lieut	Coppin A D		4346	Sgt	Dodds G	Jpn
4347	Pte	Corneck W K		2542	Bdr	Dragon C N	
3491	L/Bdr	Corra H		3737	L/Cpl	Drewery J W	Jpn
DR 23	Gnr	Cotton J A		4355	Gnr	Dreyer H	
	Pte	Cottrell G	Jpn	2105	Cpl	Drown E C	Jpn
2419	CQMS	Coulson E W	Jpn	4069	BQMS	Dudman W F	Jpn
4286	Gnr	Coxhead G S	Jpn	4102	Pte	Duffield W	Jpn
DR 8	Pte	Coxhill L F	Jpn		Cpl	Dunlop R P	
4498	Pte	Crabb F		DR 264	Gnr	Dunn L	Jpn
4267	Pte	Crary D	Jpn	2098	Pte	Dunnett F F A	Jpn
DR 57	Gnr	Crawford A K	Jpn	3650	BSM	Dupuy J T	
2138	Sgt	Crawford G W K			Pte	Durand R	
4418	Spr	Cropley C M	Jpn		Major	Durran J	
	Pte	Cross A		5283	Gnr	Dybdahl P	Jpn
	Capt	Crozier D J S		2198	Pte	Dyer W J	Jpn
2488	Pte	Cruz A R	Jpn	782	Pte	Eastman A L G	Jpn
3195	Pte	Cruz A R S	Jpn		Gnr	Edge W F	
3825	Gnr	Cruz R M	Jpn	3861	L/Bdr	Edwards G S	Jpn
4207	Pte	Cruz T J	Jpn	1765	CSM	Edwards R A	Jpn
2866	Pte	Cullen F	Jpn		Capt	Egal R	Jpn
	Lieut	Cunha E L		2418	Pte	Elarte L A	
4033	Gnr	Cunningham E S	Jpn	4550	Pte	Ellis F M	

Prisoners of War at the Time of the Japanese Surrender

No	Rank	Name		No	Rank	Name	
4832	Gnr	Ellison E	Jpn		Lieut	Geer R G	
DR 320	Pte	Engelbrecht F A	Jpn	3141	Sgm	Gegg W S	Jpn
4499	Sgm	Engelbrecht P J	Jpn	2347	Pte	Gelman B A	Jpn
3303	Gnr	Engelbrecht R J	Jpn	2829	L/Cpl	Gibson L A	
	Pte	Erskine W		3564	Pte	Gill A H	Jpn
2054	CSM	Everest R J V	Jpn	4072	Pte	Gill F A	
	Pte	Everett A G		812	BSM	Gillard A	
4839	Spr	Fallon J	Jpn	2216	L/Cpl	Glendenning L J S	Jpn
3283	Pte	Fallon P	Jpn	5245	Pte	Goldenberg A E	Jpn
4986	Spr	Fallon P	Jpn		Capt	Goldman L	
3404	Sgt	Fasciato V V	Jpn	3053	Cpl	Gomes A E	
	Lieut	Ferguson G P		4724	Spr	Gomes J V	
3890	Gnr	Ferguson J J	Jpn	4073	Pte	Gonsalves H F	
4417	Sgt	Ferguson M		DR 220	Pte	Goodban G A	
3361	Pte	Ferreira N G	Jpn	3217	Pte	Gosano G N	
	Lieut	Field B C		3710	Pte	Gosano J M	Jpn
3569	L/Cpl	Figueiredo E A	Jpn	3335	Pte	Gosano L G	
1878	CQMS	Fincher E C	Jpn	4633	L/Bdr	Gould T J	Jpn
4097	Pte	Fisher A E		4865	Sgt	Greenburg W W	
3807	Sgt	Fisher A L			Pte	Greenhalgh W E	
DR 50	Pte	Fisher E J	Jpn	4362	Pte	Gregory L R	Jpn
4642	Pte	Fisher J A	Jpn	DR 109	Pte	Gregory R F	Jpn
DR 161	Pte	Fisher W D	Jpn		Lieut	Grey G W	
5189	Gnr	Fitzhenry J K	Jpn	3806	Sgt	Griffin W G	
	Major	Flippance F		1085	Cpl	Groome E L	Jpn
3265	L/Cpl	Fonseca J C	Jpn	757	Pte	Groves W M	
DR 101	Pte	Ford J N	Jpn	1538	Sgt	Gubbay H E	
2587	Pte	Forrow K W		4823	Gnr	Gundesen J C A	
1705	L/Cpl	Fountain H J		2164	L/Sgt	Guterres G A	
2178	Pte	Fowler E A W	Jpn	5190	Gnr	Guthrie J C	Jpn
4030	L/Cpl	Fowler F A	Jpn	2720	Pte	Gutierrez E M	
1778	Cpl	Fowler S A	Jpn	3589	Pte	Gutierrez G M	
5407	Pte	Franco A V		2430	Pte	Gutierrez M M	
4109	Spr	Frenkel J		1970	Pte	Gutierrez R M	
3696	Pte	Fuertes D P	Jpn	3671	Cpl	Gutierrez R M B	
	Pte	Gahagan C E		4526	Pte	Guttierrez C L	
3333	L/Cpl	Gairdner R C	Jpn	DR 258	Pte	Hailstone B	Jpn
4183	L/Cpl	Garcia F		4613	Spr	Halfter N A	
4553	Gnr	Garcia H A	Jpn	4227	Pte	Hall E S	
3130	L/Cpl	Garcia W A	Jpn	2857	Sgt	Hall G A V	
3317	Gnr	Gardner A G	Jpn	4687	Pte	Halsall H	Jpn
3468	Spr	Gardner W A	Jpn	3304	Sgm	Hamilton D H	Jpn
3034	Pte	Gardner W J F			Capt	Hamilton K C	
	Major	Garland N		4318	L/Cpl	Hammond N G	Jpn
3857	Cpl	Gavriloff G J			Cpl	Hance J H R	
3805	Sgt	Geall W J			Pte	Hanna F H	

Prisoners of War at the Time of the Japanese Surrender

No	Rank	Name		No	Rank	Name	
3647	BQMS	Harkins M J		3177	Cpl	Jaffer N	
4754	Gnr	Harrop G		4388	L/Cpl	Jamieson C V	
3750	Pte	Harrop J W			Major	Jarvis S	
4315	L/Bdr	Hart-Davis J A V	Jpn	3804	Sgt	Jeffreys A C	
4513	Sgt	Hatt C		3414	Spr	Jelihovsky G N	
4403	Pte	Haynes G	Jpn		Pte	Jesus J M	Jpn
4199	CSM	Henderson G		4373	Pte	Jiricek A	
4824	Pte	Henkin B W		5405	Pte	Joanilho A	Jpn
4867	Gnr	Henningsen F F	Jpn		Pte	Joffe E M	Jpn
2815	Sgt	Herdman G L				Joffe E M	Jpn
3454	RQMS	Hewitt W		2382	Sgt	Johnsen J O	
	Pte	Heywood G S P	Jpn	1121	Sgt	Johnson G E L	
4126	Pte	Hicks H J		3868	Pte	Johnstone A C	
	Capt	Hill S O		4229	Gnr	Jolendovsky T A	Jpn
3628	Spr	Hill W R		6137055	RSM	Jones F C	
2654	Sgt	Hillon F	Jpn	4991	Gnr	Jones J G	
	Pte	Hingston H		2999	L/Cpl	Jones R F K	Jpn
1359	L/Cpl	Hirst W H G	Jpn	5241	Gnr	Jonge G De	Jpn
DR 138	Sgt	Hitchins W E F		3124	Pte	Jorge A V	Jpn
4723	Sgt	Hoare R E		DR 115	Pte	Kaluzhny K A	
4503	Pte	Hollands F W	Jpn	3186	Pte	Kaploon B L	
3726	Gnr	Holm J		3185	Cpl	Karpusheff G	Jpn
	Pte	Hong B		3271	L/Cpl	Keeble J H	
2158	Sgt	Hopkins H F	Jpn	DR 240	Pte	Keen K L	Jpn
	Pte	Horowitz J H		DR 257	Pte	Kees H O	Jpn
4120	Cpl	Houston W		DR 75	Gnr	Kelly G	
3665	Sgt	Howard W J	Jpn	3152	Pte	Kempton J	Jpn
5311	Gnr	Howell I H	Jpn	374	RQMS	Kew A E	Jpn
4726	Pte	Huber T	Jpn	DR 285	Pte	Kim N	Jpn
1796	CSM	Hume L W		5524	Sgm	King J J O	Jpn
4312	Bdr	Humfrey L H G	Jpn	2953	Gnr	King T H W	Jpn
DR 176	Pte	Hunt H C		3808	CSM	Kirkwood R	Jpn
2055	Sgt	Hurlow L A	Jpn	4725	Pte	Knight H C D	Jpn
3552	Pte	Hutchinson D A	Jpn	3880	Pte	Knox D H	Jpn
3879	Pte	Hutchison A C		2373	Cpl	Knox W T	Jpn
DR 60	Pte	Hutchison J		3634	Pte	Komorsky A	
4356	Gnr	Huttemeier E E		4374	Pte	Krofta J	
3544	Sgt	Hyde W	Jpn	DR 131	Cpl	Labrousse E D	
2585	L/Cpl	Hynes D A	Jpn	2761	CQMS	Labrum G B	
DR 206	L/Cpl	Iles W J		2612	CQMS	Labrum V C	
1747	Pte	Ingram T R	Jpn		Cpl	Lamb W G	Jpn
3137	Pte	Irving F H		2658	L/Bdr	Landau L	
3496	Pte	Itenson V A	Jpn		Capt	Langenberg C van	
	Pte	Ivers J E	Jpn	4521	Pte	Lapsley A W	Jpn
3654	Pte	Izatt D B	Jpn	4522	Pte	Lapsley F M	Jpn
5048	Pte	Jack C G			Lieut	Lapsley R	

Prisoners of War at the Time of the Japanese Surrender

No	Rank	Name		No	Rank	Name	
2838	Pte	Lapsley R H A	Jpn	4684	Gnr	MacKenzie N H	Jpn
4381	Spr	Lay F J			Lieut	MacKichan A S	
3183	Lieut	Lebedeff A		2747	Cpl	Madar T A	Jpn
	Pte	Lee		3666	Spr	Maher B A	
DR 55	L/Bdr	Lee A T			Spr	Maker	
4536	Gnr	Lee E F		4982	Pte	Manley J C	
DR 38	Pte	Lee F		3655	Pte	Manson C J	Jpn
2757	Gnr	Lee J H B		3829	Gnr	Marcal BA	Jpn
4132	Spr	Lee R	Jpn	3594	Pte	Marcal J V H	Jpn
DR 82	L/Cpl	Lee R E		2845	Pte	Marques E S	Jpn
2697	CQMS	Leigh R	Jpn	3167	Pte	Marques J A	Jpn
2564	Cpl	Leitch J R		3711	Pte	Marques L G	
4271	L/Bdr	Leonard A R		3673	Pte	Marques L Z	
2503	L/Sgt	Leonard D J	Jpn	3869	Pte	Marriott H E	Jpn
2628	Gnr	Leonard N L	Jpn	3135	L/Cpl	Marrs G M	Jpn
2504	Pte	Leonard S L	Jpn	4350	Gnr	Marshal G L	Jpn
3894	L/Cpl	Leonard T A	Jpn	2145	Pte	Marshall A	
4727	Sgm	Le Patourel C B	Jpn		Pte	Martland L	Jpn
3757	L/Cpl	Le Tissier P J	Jpn	3648	L/Bdr	Marton O E C	
4029	Cpl	Levy J F		DR 293	L/Cpl	Mathias E G	Jpn
4034	Gnr	Lewis A J	Jpn	4707	Gnr	Mathias H A	Jpn
4184	Bdr	Lloyd-Jones E		DR 123	Pte	Matthews C N	Jpn
4100	Gnr	Lock A		4523	Pte	Matthews E N	Jpn
DR 10	Cpl	Lock T	Jpn	4717	Gnr	Maughan S L	Jpn
3308	Gnr	Lockhart T L	Jpn	2967	S/Sgt	Maunder F G	Jpn
1200	Sgt	Logan C R		4524	Sgm	Maycock E R	Jpn
3225	Sgt	Lomeav G A (alias Lemay)		5402	Pte	Maycock J H	Jpn
DR 247	Pte	Loncraine D C		3553	Pte	Maycock R J	
2699	L/Cpl	Long H K		3626	Pte	Maycock W G	Jpn
4045	L/Bdr	Long W G	Jpn	2816	Sgt	McColgan D	Jpn
3590	Pte	Lopes C L		DR 139	Pte	McCombe W W	Jpn
3591	Cpl	Lopes D F			Cpl	McCurrach W J	Jpn
3592	Pte	Lopes D V		DR 315	Pte	McDonald J W	Jpn
4287	Gnr	Low T B	Jpn	DR 261	Pte	McKay H A	
4408	Pte	Lowe W	Jpn	DR 99	Pte	McKellar A	
3846	Cpl	Lowrie J		4333	Sgt	McKelvie J	
	Gnr	Lui T C			Pte	McKenna T S	
2227	Pte	Luz J A da			Lieut	McLellan D	
3645	Pte	Luz J V da		4199	Pte	McMaster W D	
4370	L/Bdr	Mabb A	Jpn	4121	Pte	McPherson J	Jpn
2994	Cpl	MacFarlane W E	Jpn	1461	Sgt	Meadows R S	Jpn
2051	Sgt	MacFayden A J		4407	Pte	Melville G	Jpn
DR 295	Pte	MacIntyre J L	Jpn	1920	CQMS	Meyer J G	
	Pte	Mackay H S		4342	Pte	Miller E P	Jpn
1957	Sgt	MacKay J F C	Jpn	854	CSM	Millington H J	
4133	L/Cpl	MacKenzie H L	Jpn	2103	Sgt	Millington L C	Jpn

No	Rank	Name		No	Rank	Name	
2357	Pte	Millington V J		3234	Pte	Parsons D O	Jpn
	Lt Col	Mitchell E J R			Capt	Parsons T R	
DR 309	Pte	Mitchell J G	Jpn	DR 121	L/Cpl	Partridge F K	Jpn
3229	Sgm	Mitchell J V G	Jpn	3870	Pte	Paterson G W	Jpn
3634	Sgt	Mitchell K	Jpn		Major	Paterson J J	
3208	Sgt	Monks B J M		3410	Sgt	Pattern P K M	Jpn
4424	Cpl	Moors H L			Pte	Paul A F	
DR 122	Gnr	Morgan L G	Jpn		Spr	Pavloff A V	
4204	Pte	Morgenstern N		3086	Bdr	Peaker A J	Jpn
4103	Sgt	Morrison C G M		DR 13	Gnr	Pearne J R A	Jpn
4200	Cpl	Morrison R		DR 141	Cpl	Pearse H V	
1324	Sgt	Moses E S		4123	Sgt	Pearson A E	
DR 110	Cpl	Murphy E O		3363	Gnr	Pedersen K W	
2601	Sgt	Murphy J P	Jpn		Capt	Penn A H A	
3142	Pte	Musker L	Jpn	2097	Cpl	Pereira A P Jr	Jpn
3323	Sgt	Muskett W H B			Pte	Pereira C C	
4527	Gnr	Naess B R		3602	Pte	Pereira J A	Jpn
3482	Spr	Napoloff A I		3603	Pte	Pereira R L	
2818	Sgt	Needham C F	Jpn	4344	Gnr	Peresypkin O P	Jpn
3175	L/Cpl	Nelson K B	Jpn		Lieut	Perry A E	
5234	Pte	Nesteroff M J		4515	Pte	Perry E W	
3696	Pte	Neves A C	Jpn	3630	Pte	Petrove M	
3144	SQMS	Newton E A R	Jpn	DR 166	Sgt	Piercy G H	
	Lieut	Nigel F G		3785	L/Cpl	Pinna C L	
491	Piper	Nisbet G		1480	Sgt	Pinna G A de	
3701	Pte	Noronha A A		4626	L/Cpl	Pinna H R de	
2812	L/Cpl	Noronha A E		2001	Cpl	Pinna L G	
4056	Pte	Noronha A F	Jpn	940	Gnr	Pomeroy J B	
3597	Pte	Noronha E A	Jpn	2301	CSM	Poole S G	Jpn
3674	Cpl	Noronha G A		3604	Pte	Prata A J M	Jpn
3598	Cpl	Noronha H A	Jpn	2681	L/Cpl	Prettejohn J P	Jpn
4325	Pte	Novikov V A		4379	Spr	Prish R	
1595	Pte	Nunes V M			Lieut	Prophet D L	
DR 106	Gnr	O' Connor M G		DR 267	Sgt	Provan J D	
3437	Bdr	O' Connor W	Jpn	DR 284	Gnr	Pullen W P	Jpn
5189	Gnr	O' Grady J H	Jpn	DR 16	Gnr	Railton E W	
3466	L/Bdr	Oliver G H	Jpn	4167	S/Sgt	Rakusen M N	Jpn
4630	Gnr	Ongstad L H A	Jpn	DR 273	L/Cpl	Ramsay J V	
4361	Pte	Orchard W D			Capt	Ramsey	
4706	Pte	Ostroumoff A		3715	Spr	Ramsey W L	
4066	BSM	Oswald L G	Jpn	DR 326	Pte	Rance A W	Jpn
	Pte	Owens R A		4124	Pte	Randle J A B	Jpn
2487	Pte	Ozorio G M		4635	Pte	Read J	Jpn
	Lieut	Palmer G T			Lieut	Redman J	
2737	L/Cpl	Parker R G			Major	Redmond F A	
		Parkus R L	Jpn	DR 4	L/Bdr	Reed R C	

Prisoners of War at the Time of the Japanese Surrender

No	Rank	Name		No	Rank	Name	
3556	Pte	Reed R J		3813	Pte	Rodrigues L M	
	Capt	Rees G F		3193	Pte	Rootstein A	
3391	Pte	Reis F W	Jpn		Pte	Roscoe J	
3568	Pte	Remedios A A dos			Col	Rose H B	Jpn
1223	Pte	Remedios A L V	Jpn	2667	BSM	Rose H H	
4209	Pte	Remedios A M		DR 67	Gnr	Ross G R	Jpn
3607	Cpl	Remedios C F	Jpn	3871	L/Cpl	Rosselet C S	Jpn
1190	Pte	Remedios E A V	Jpn	5243	Sgm	Rowe A W	Jpn
3302	Pte	Remedios E E dos	Jpn	4859	Pte	Rowe G T	Jpn
4516	Cpl	Remedios H C		2196	L/Cpl	Roylance G E K	Jpn
3639	L/Cpl	Remedios H M		4060	Pte	Roza A A da	
4058	Cpl	Remedios J A		2179	L/Cpl	Roza C A da	Jpn
2223	Sgt	Remedios J C	Jpn	3324	Pte	Roza E D da	Jpn
1293	Sgt	Remedios J D dos	Jpn	2463	Sgt	Roza M K	Jpn
3125	Pte	Remedios J F		3601	Pte	Roza-Pereira C E	
2170	Pte	Remedios J J		3612	Pte	Rozario C L	Jpn
4082	Gnr	Remedios L A R		3171	Sgt	Rush J P	Jpn
2726	Cpl	Remedios L G D'A			Lieut	Russell J	
3813	Pte	Remedios L M		1592	CQMS	Sa H de	
3786	Pte	Remedios M A D'A			Pte	Saladin G	
4517	Pte	Remidios P D'A		3356	Sgm	Salter C L	Jpn
4419	Gnr	Reynolds J		DR 273	Pte	Samuel P E H	Jpn
5238	Pte	Ribeiro A E V			Pte	Sandford J M	Jpn
1323	Cpl	Ribeiro C A de J V	Jpn	3642	Pte	Santos C M	Jpn
3619	Pte	Ribeiro C de M C V		2982	Pte	Santos F J	
3501	Pte	Ribeiro E J		3191	Lieut	Schiller G J	
	Lieut	Ribeiro F V V		4996	Pte	Schiller M J	
2479	Pte	Ribeiro H A	Jpn	DR 184	L/Cpl	Scicluna C G	
3269	Pte	Ribeiro H J	Jpn	4265	Pte	Scicluna F D	
3611	Pte	Ribeiro J F V	Jpn		Lieut	Scott H H	
4210	Pte	Ribeiro L F V	Jpn	5000	Pte	Scott W	
4548	Gnr	Ribeiro L G V	Jpn	3205	Sgm	Semmelman C J	
3677	Pte	Ribeiro L M V		3573	Pte	Sequeira C M	Jpn
2478	Pte	Ribeiro R M V	Jpn	2091	L/Cpl	Sequeira J O	
4360	Gnr	Riertsen R	Jpn	3703	Pte	Sequeira M H	
4551	Pte	Roberts E A		3614	Pte	Sequeira V A da C	Jpn
	Capt	Roberts R A		3212	Gnr	Seyer K D	Jpn
	Major	Robertson C de S		2713	Pte	Shaw J A	Jpn
DR 168	Pte	Robertson E K			Pte	Shaw J H	
4046	Gnr	Robertson F A		4261	L/Cpl	Shea J F	Jpn
	Capt	Robertson K S		2990	L/Cpl	Sheehan B	
3693	Pte	Robertson W G		2948	Sgt	Sherriff G H	Jpn
3439	Gnr	Rocha C L	Jpn		Major	Sherry J P	
3438	Gnr	Rocha FL	Jpn	5003	Pte	Shihwarg A S	
	Capt	Rodrigues A M		3238	L/Cpl	Sills C A	Jpn
	Capt	Rodrigues J S		1680	L/Cpl	Silva C M da	

Prisoners of War at the Time of the Japanese Surrender

No	Rank	Name	
2407	Pte	Silva E J	
2834	Pte	Silva G V da	Jpn
3575	Pte	Silva L C	
4084	L/Cpl	Silva L J da	
3576	Pte	Silva L M	
2431	L/Cpl	Silva M C M	Jpn
1089	L/Cpl	Silva M M	
	Lieut	Silva P M N da	
2183	Pte	Silva R D	Jpn
2402	L/Cpl	Silva R M da	Jpn
4085	Pte	Silva R M da	Jpn
962	Pte	Silva S R da	
3574	Pte	Silva; L A	
3809	Sgt	Simmons B W	
1795	L/Cpl	Simpson R A J	
1258	Cpl	Simpson W C	
4326	Gnr	Sinclair D B	
	Pte	Singh H	
4999	Gnr	Skinner O	
	Lieut	Skvorzov A V	
	Lieut	Sleap R	
2629	Cpl	Sleap S A	
2219	Sgm	Sloan C M	Jpn
	Pte	Sloan J K	Jpn
5174	Gnr	Sloss G	Jpn
4316	Gnr	Smeby N W	
DR 54	Pte	Smirke F H	
2859	Pte	Smirke L E	Jpn
3792	Bdr	Smith A	
5257	CQMS	Smith A J V	
1982	Cpl	Smith D T	Jpn
	Major	Smith J	
3305	Sgm	Smith N L	
	Pte	Smith R W	Jpn
2162	Cpl	Soares C E	Jpn
3616	Pte	Soares F M	
2717	Pte	Soares H A	
2421	Pte	Soares L A	
1600	Cpl	Soares M M de V	
5222	Gnr	Solecki J	Jpn
DR 228	Pte	Sollis C G	
3577	Pte	Sousa S S	
3213	Pte	Souza H A	Jpn
2157	CSM	Souza J T P	Jpn
3679	Pte	Souza L A	Jpn
2840	Pte	Souza R A	Jpn

No	Rank	Name	
	Lieut	Spary A	
3772	Cpl	Spoors A D	Jpn
3461	Sgt	Spoov A V	
1906	Pte	Sprague W	
3309	CSM	Stainton T F	
4375	Pte	Stanek F	Jpn
2050	CQMS	Steven A	
	Major	Stewart E G	
3631	Gnr	Stewart H G	Jpn
DR 253	Pte	Stewart H R	
	Lieut	Stoker W	
	Capt	Strellet D L	
3139	Sgm	Suiter T M H	Jpn
DR 323	Cpl	Sullivan I G	
4870	Pte	Sully A K	Jpn
3143	Gnr	Swan M M	Jpn
	Lieut	Sweeney J N	
3321	CQMS	Sykes L	Jpn
4709	Pte	Tadema-Wielandt H J	Jpn
4665	Pte	Talbot B	
	Lieut	Tamworth I P	
4737	Gnr	Tandy E J	Jpn
	Pte	Tappenden H H	
2947	Pte	Tate A	Jpn
4564	Pte	Taudien C H	Jpn
4309	Sgt	Tausz J	Jpn
4211	Pte	Taylor A J G	Jpn
	Pte	Taylor R B	
	Lieut	Tebbutt H J	
DR 183	Pte	Thirlwell J W	Jpn
	Pte	Thomas J C	
	Sgt	Thompson	
DR 56	Pte	Thompson C	Jpn
	Pte	Thompson E	
3036	Cpl	Thompson F M	Jpn
3077	BQMS	Thomson F S	Jpn
	Major	Thursby E N	
1095	Pte	Tillery W C	
	Pte	Tinson A C	Jpn
3872	Pte	Tocher J E	Jpn
4398	Sgt	Tollan D	
4369	Gnr	Tomes K	Jpn
4698	Cpl	Townley A N	
		(alias Tonoff)	
3182	Gnr	Tsenin E A	
3839	Sgt	Tuck E	

Prisoners of War at the Time of the Japanese Surrender

No	Rank	Name		No	Rank	Name	
DR 104	Gnr	Tucker N F	Jpn	1321	Sgm	Whitley T S D	Jpn
4708	Gnr	Upton V G H	Jpn		Lieut	Wilby G S	
	Capt	Valentine R K		DR 266	Pte	Wilkinson H W	Jpn
2989	Sgt	Vargasoff N		DR 160	Pte	Wilkinson W R J	Jpn
4111	Sgt	Venshou A C		4376	Sgt	Williams E H	Jpn
3621	Pte	Victor C de M C			Major	Williams H G	
3622	L/Cpl	Victor J A		DR 113	Gnr	Williamson H N	
3811	L/Bdr	Villa Carlos M	Jpn	3578	Pte	Williamson W	Jpn
5403	Pte	Voronkin D			Lieut	Willy C	
2380	Gnr	Voronoff C V			Lieut	Wilson J M	
	Capt	Waddell C J		5228	Pte	Wilson W M	Jpn
3554	Pte	Waid J	Jpn	1703	Sgt	Winch G S	Jpn
3076	Sgt	Walker C D N	Jpn	2244	L/Cpl	Winyard J R	
2709	Pte	Walker D	Jpn	DR 243	Pte	Wolosh C M	Jpn
3548	CQMS	Walker G F	Jpn	DR 71	Cpl	Wood E C	Jpn
3845	Pte	Walker J E Y	Jpn		Capt	Wood G G	
	Lt Col	Walker R D		2003	Pte	Woolley H J	
4695	Gnr	Walree E van			Lieut	Wright A M J	
4048	Gnr	Ward A S		3393	Pte	Xavier A C	Jpn
3854	Pte	Ward J E			Pte	Xavier A F	
3549	Sgt	Warnes T A		3820	L/Cpl	Xavier A M	Jpn
	Major	Watson J		4552	Pte	Xavier A P	Jpn
4094	Gnr	Watson R A E	Jpn	3725	Pte	Xavier C M de P	
	Capt	Way J R		3623	Pte	Xavier H J	
3539	Gnr	Webb R L S		3460	Pte	Xavier J H	Jpn
5175	Gnr	Weller F A	Jpn	4540	Sgt	Xavier L A	Jpn
4623	Pte	White A H	Jpn	3624	Gnr	Xavier RA	
2773	BQMS	White A W T	Jpn	5227	Gnr	Yaholkovsky G A	
4170	Pte	White G A	Jpn	3359	Cpl	Yatskin M C	
1886	Sgt	White G J	Jpn	DR 76	Cpl	Young K P	Jpn
1305	Pte	White J P	Jpn	4192	L/Bdr	Yourieff E G	
1759	CSM	White V H	Jpn	3625	Cpl	Yvanovich P A Jr	
3085	Arm/S/Sgt	White W D		2870	L/Bdr	Zaitzeff A	Jpn
DR 316	Spr	Whiting C W	Jpn	5401	Pte	Zimmerman	

Interned in the Stanley Civilian Internment Camp

No	Rank	Name	No	Rank	Name
	Pte	Ashby R J		Pte	Langston A G
1789	CSM	Begg S O		Cpl	Leiper G A
	Pte	Blumenthall L		Sgt	Linaker J
5308	Sgt	Brown L R		Pte	Littler C
	Pte	Burns J E		Pte	Loseby F H
	Pte	Butler R C		Pte	Lucock E J
	Pte	Cox A R		Pte	Lunny J F
	Pte	Crofton C C F		Pte	Lyle J
	Pte	Davis J C	2087	Pte	MacKenzie A W
	Pte	De Rome L	4711	Gnr	Mardulyn R P
4646	Sgt	Dixon V C		Pte	Marvin S H
	Pte	Duckworth F F		Pte	McCutcheon J
3889	Spr	Evans G		Pte	McDonald C T F
	Lieut	Fitzgerald J W		Pte	McGrath G W
	Pte	Fitzgerald R C		Pte	McTavich L J
	Pte	Floyde W H		Pte	Mitchell A M
	Pte	Fordham L J		Lieut	Norman C J
2004	Sgt	Foster A		Pte	Orchard W E
4729	Cpl	Fox J A		Pte	Padgett G T
	Pte	Franks E S		Cpl	Plumb B
	Pte	Gemmell G		Pte	Rae F L
	Pte	Gibson L		Pte	Randall H V C
	Pte	Grant J W		Pte	Robertson R G
	Pte	Grindley R J V		Pte	Rosen R S
	Sgt	Grinter E		Pte	Schouten K
3540	Cpl	Halligan G		Sgt	Sharp E W
	Pte	Haynes C W		Pte	Shotton G B
	Pte	Hill F N	1891	Pte	Stark C C
	Pte	Hircock A W		Pte	Stevens E
	Pte	Hodge S		Pte	Stonehouse W
	Sgt	Hudson J W		Pte	Stuart J S B B
3530	Sgt	Humphrey E G K		Pte	Tarbuck A P
3877	Pte	Humphries W G		Pte	Thomson G G
	Capt	Hutton-Potts A		Pte	Vanthal H M
	Pte	Johnson G		Pte	Venables A C
	Pte	Jones R E		Pte	Ward W
	Pte	Joyce J S		Pte	Webber W E
	Pte	Kingdon C J	2954	Sgm	Wilson B S
3667	Pte	Koodiaroff M A		Pte	Winterton F T
	Pte	Krogh-Moe J		Pte	Woodward G

Released by the Japanese

No	Rank	Name	No	Rank	Name
4704	Pte	Amplavanar S	4392	Pte	Lam Ping Kee
4755	Pte	Au Sze Ho	5041	Pte	Lau Hun Ming
3295	Pte	Au Young R	2486	Gnr	Lau J A
3216	L/Bdr	Bakar A H	5042	Pte	Lau Teik Seng
2333	Gnr	Bucks R	DR 46	Spr	Lay W
2330	Gnr	Bucks S	4726	Pte	Lee Chi Nam
4088	Gnr	Chan A	3423	Gnr	Lee Chun Chung
5050	Pte	Chan Ah Kheng	4875	Pte	Lee Gordon Chun
2659	L/Bdr	Chan C	4802	Pte	Lee How Fong
3492	Gnr	Chan Chi Wing	5010	Pte	Lee Wee Son
3470	L/Bdr	Chan Hoi Kee	5056	Pte	Leow Hock Yew
3488	Gnr	Chan Kwong Luen	2632	Gnr	Leung J
5051	Pte	Cheah Phee Chuan	5192	Gnr	Leung K S
5014	Pte	Chelliah D	3165	Pte	Leung Nai Sung
5180	Gnr	Cheng Po Yee	4694	Pte	Leung Po Shun
5173	Pte	Cheung J	4384	Gnr	Li A
4110	Pte	Cheung Shiu Ling	4804	Pte	Lim Thiam Tet
3373	L/Cpl	Cheung T	5188	Gnr	Lo Hon Sang
2800	Gnr	Cheung Yan Sing	4272	Gnr	Lo Ka Mo
5006	Pte	Chiang Lee Hin	4747	Pte	Lo Shu Wing
5046	Pte	Chin H	4692	Pte	Lo Yau Sam
5052	Pte	Chin Yew Ping	5057	Pte	Loh Tat Beng
3824	Gnr	Choy Chung Lun	5043	Pte	Low Keat Soo
5007	Pte	Dasen A	3395	Pte	Lui Kwai Hong
4137	Gnr	Eng Wah Sun	5012	Pte	Lung Li Shih
DR277	Pte	Fenton J C	5113	Pte	Maddan D R
4138	Gnr	Fong S	4757	Pte	Mahmood Syed
3207	Pte	Gill R S	4518	Gnr	Markar A K
2882	L/S	Goh Kim Toon	4519	Gnr	Markar E R
	Pte	Hausammann E		Pte	Master R J
4648	Gnr	Ho Chai Nam	3422	Gnr	Mok Hing Woon
4762	Pte	Ho F	5088	Pte	Moung Ba Sin
5004	Pte	Ho Mang Hung	4078	L/Cpl	Nanak E B
5008	Pte	Hor Ah Lam	2335	Gnr	Nanak H A
4629	Gnr	Hoy Poy B H A		Pte	Ng Jit Thye
2649	Sgt	Hu Kwok Leung	5218	Gnr	Nguyuen L
3472	Gnr	Ip Wing	2555	Gnr	Omar A K
2541	Gnr	Ismail A H	3436	Gor	Pau C F S
4220	Pte	Jacob A R	4080	Pte	Paul H P
5111	Pte	Khoo Kay Hean	3494	L/Bdr	Poon Chun Ho
5187	Gnr	Khor Suan Sin	4422	Pte	Poon O A
5009	Pte	Koh Jaik Chong	3425	Bdr	Pun Yiu Kwan
2880	Gnr	Kwok Chan Lun	4232	Gnr	Rum Yee D
3827	Gnr	Kwok Kap Lun	4203	Pte	Rumjahn A K
4240	Gnr	Kwok Ling Kwong	5186	Sgm	Sammy M
4658	Gnr	Lai J	5053	Pte	Seah Tin Toon

Released by the Japanese

No	Rank	Name	No	Rank	Name
2828	Gnr	Seemin A H	2949	Sgm	Wong Kam Piu
4993	Spr	Shek W	4190	Gnr	Wong Kwai Yan
5013	Pte	Sim Beck Ho	4049	L/Cpl	Wong Kwok Suen
5087	Pte	Singh Naranjan	4987	Spr	Wong Yee A D
4710	Pte	Tam Chung Man	5055	Pte	Wong Yin Knoon
5044	Pte	Tan Boon Cheok	4811	Pte	Wong Yue Tin
5045	Pte	Tan Ewe Aik	4763	Pte	Yap Pitt Van
5082	Pte	Tan Yok Lin	3276	Pte	Yeung Wing
3481	Gnr	Tang Sik Hung	5183	Sgm	Yoong G
5114	Pte	Vengadasalam P	4980	Pte	Young B J
2543	Bdr	Wahab A M	2371	Pte	Zimmern A
5223	Gnr	Wan Hok Nin	4259	Pte	Zimmern F
5054	Pte	Wen Chung Wen	2423	L/Cpl	Zimmern F R

Did Not Enter POW Camps or Escaped in Early 1942

No	Rank	Name	No	Rank	Name
3435	Bdr	Ali E	4245	Spr	Chan H H
3583	Pte	Aquino D L d'		Pte	Chan H M
	Pte	Au Kim Wah	2862	Pte	Chan H Y
3347	L/Cpl	Au Ping Wah	3282	Pte	Chan Hiu Chung
2942	Pte	Au Sze Bun	2861	Pte	Chan Hon Cheung
4388	Pte	Au Yang K S	3072	L/Cpl	Chan Iu Tung
3129	Pte	Baptista R C	3822	Gnr	Chan Kai Hung
3669	Pte	Botelho H A	2917	Gnr	Chan Kang Chuen
4399	L/Cpl	Braga A M	2995	L/Cpl	Chan King Chor
3513	Spr	Brasilevsky E D	4292	Gnr	Chan Kwai
	Major	Bunje F	4219	Pte	Chan Kwong Fook
2961	Sgt	Burke S	3487	Gnr	Chan L
	Pte	Burns R K		Spr	Chan Lam
2836	Pte	Carmo A F	4705	Gnr	Chan P
2780	Pte	Castilho Q A	3449	Gnr	Chan Pui Kan
4931	Gnr	Castro F A	4558	Gnr	Chan S K
4241	Pte	Chai Kim Swee		Spr	Chan Shing
4546	Gnr	Chan	3426	Gnr	Chan Sik Tim
3000	Pte	Chan A Kung Po	4742	Pte	Chan Siu Lun
3045	L/S	Chan Cheuk Kwan		Spr	Chan Wing
3013	Cpl	Chan Chi Fat	4810	Pte	Chan Yan Kwong
	Spr	Chan Chou	4386	L/Bdr	Chang W Shin Fook
3088	Sgm	Chan F	5073	Sgm	Cheah Chong Kee
3823	Gnr	Chan Fook Cheung	2957	Sgm	Chen J Ming
2996	Pte	Chan Fook Chor		Spr	Cheng Chi Man
3078	Pte	Chan Fook Kang		Spr	Cheung Chung Hong
	Pte	Chan H		Pte	Cheung H

Did Not Enter POW Camps or Escaped in Early 1942

No	Rank	Name	No	Rank	Name
4412	Pte	Cheung Koon Ming		Pte	Fung Ki Wui
4672	Pte	Cheung Kwok Yan	2915	Pte	Fung Y S
5005	Pte	Cheung Man Wah	3493	Gnr	Fung Yin Leung
4756	Pte	Cheung Ming Wah	4054	Pte	Gaan C A
	Cpl	Cheung Shu Tung	2892	L/Cpl	Goh Kong Hooi
	Spr	Cheung Yau	3709	Pte	Gomes J J
3121	Pte	Cheung Yim Sang	DR 77	Pte	Gordon G A
	Pte	Chevillard M	4512	Pte	Gosano B T
5086	Pte	Chew Beng Kheng		Pte	Heiberg S K
5165	Gnr	Chiang Lee Hai	3421	Gnr	Heung L
5181	Pte	Chin H T	3247	Pte	Ho C
4615	Gnr	Ching A	3253	Pte	Ho Chung Yin
4693	Pte	Chiu Put Chi	3044	Pte	Ho Kwai Wing
4743	Pte	Chow Cham Leung		Spr	Ho Lam
4136	Bdr	Chow G L	4872	Pte	Ho T
	Pte	Chow H S		Pte	Hoe A S
4270	Gnr	Chow Kwai Cheong	4801	Pte	Hooi Cheng Weng
	Pte	Chow S	5089	Pte	Huang C L
3041	L/Cpl	Chow Yau Cheung	3266	Pte	Hui Chung Fat
	Spr	Chow Yuk Sang	2684	Spr	Ing W Sui
2889	Pte	Chow Yung	2893	Pte	Ip Iu Ting
5181	Pte	Chu Hing To		Spr	Ip King
3476	L/Bdr	Chu Kam Yin	4701	Pte	Ip Tai Cheung
4387	Gnr	Chua P T H	4559	Gnr	Ip Tai Chiu
4547	Gnr	Chung A	4234	Spr	Ivaschenko N N
	Pte	Chung Chu Wah	4410	Spr	Ivaskevitch A J
	Pte	Chung Kam Hing	DR216	Pte	Jackson A
2579	Gnr	Chung R		Pte	Johnston T A
4529	Gnr	Chung Wah Cheung	3724	Pte	Jorge P T
3428	Gnr	Chung Wah Chiu		Spr	Kam Yiu
4530	Gnr	Chung Wah Kiu		Spr	Kan U Wah
4531	Gnr	Chung Wah Leung	4805	Pte	Khoo Kee Seang
	Pte	Ciardi M	5185	Sgm	Khoo O J
4071	Pte	Cruz G A da	5161	Gnr	Kwai F W
2856	Sgt	Curreen I S A	4277	Gnr	Kwok Kai Chiu
5225	Pte	Daw A J	2883	L/Cpl	Kwok Kam Lun
3201	L/Cpl	Eu W	3444	Gnr	Kwok Mok Chi
4744	Pte	Fang Sin Yang	3443	L/Bdr	Kwok Mok Hoi
3702	Pte	Figueiredo E A	2884	Cpl	Kwok Yik On
	Pte	Fisher J A	5074	Sgm	Kwong K C
4813	Pte	Fok P	4143	Gnr	Kwong M
2891	Pte	Foo Ping Yuen	4169	Pte	Lai Cho Chor
4833	Pte	Foo Yeow Khoon		Spr	Lai Chu
2876	Cpl	Fung Che Lai	2911	Pte	Lai Chun Chou
4534	Pte	Fung F	4534	Gnr	Lai Wing Yat
3043	Pte	Fung Kam Fook		Spr	Lai Yau Yick

Did Not Enter POW Camps or Escaped in Early 1942

No	Rank	Name	No	Rank	Name
	Pte	Lam Chor Man		Spr	Li Tong
3114	Pte	Lam Chun Mun	3093	Pte	Li Wing Foon
4320	Pte	Lam J	3094	Pte	Li Wing Hon
4619	Gnr	Lam J Yee	4394	Pte	Li Yun Gun
	Spr	Lam Lin	5162	Gnr	Liang Kam Yuen
3441	Gnr	Lam Po Sih	5039	Pte	Lim Beng Chey
5184	Gnr	Lam Yuk Jaak	4822	Pte	Lim Chin Lang
2811	Pte	Lam Yun Ming		Pte	Lim Eng Hooi
3519	Gnr	Landau E		Pte	Lin Ho Wah
	Sgt	Lau Cheung	5047	Pte	Lin Sin Lam
	Spr	Lau Kau	4818	Pte	Ling Tak Hong
2554	Cpl	Lau Ming Sai		Spr	Liu Heung
	Spr	Lau Ping		Spr	Liu Sum
4067	Pte	Lau Ping Kwan		Spr	Liu Ting Fai
3365	Pte	Lau Yam Choi	3371	Pte	Lo Chan Ping
	Spr	Lau Ying Lap		Pte	Lo Ford
4745	Pte	Lee B	3397	Pte	Lo Kam Kei
4091	Gnr	Lee Chor Ching		Spr	Lo Kam Ting
3071	L/Cpl	Lee Hing Cheung		Spr	Lo Kim
3120	Cpl	Lee J		Spr	Lo Kin
2894	Pte	Lee Kui Chee	4561	Gnr	Lo P S
	Pte	Lee S Y		Pte	Lo Ping Yat
DR 39	Gnr	Lee W J		Gnr	Lo S
5179	Pte	Leung Cheun Bun	4565	Gnr	Lo T S
3279	Pte	Leung Chi Chung		Spr	Lo Tat Sang
	Spr	Leung Chung Yin	4735	Pte	Lo Tung Leung
4679	Pte	Leung H		Pte	Lo W
3039	L/Cpl	Leung Hon Chuen	4829	Gnr	Lo Ying Yuen
4826	Gnr	Leung Hon Ming		Cpl	Lobertson San Pui de
	Pte	Leung Kam Lun	3430	L/Bdr	Loo Tsun Huen
2801	Cpl	Leung King Hin	4216	Pte	Lor Wing Kit
	L/Cpl	Leung S L	3059	Gnr	Lui Wai Chow
3069	Pte	Leung Shew Chow		Pte	Ma Chang Ling
4146	Gnr	Leung Shui Poi		Pte	Ma H Quonnon
3448	Gnr	Leung Tsi Wai	3490	Gnr	Ma Pui Hung
3506	Gnr	Leung Wai Tak		L/Cpl	Ma R
2895	Pte	Leung Wing Yan	3491	Gnr	Ma Shuen Hung
4211	Pte	Leung Yee Chui	3509	Gnr	Ma Siu Leong
	L/Cpl	Leung Yun Cheung	2246	Pte	MacIntosh C
4985	Gnr	Li Fai Kuen	DR242	Pte	Maitland R J
	Spr	Li Hon Ki	5258	Spr	Milenko B G
4090	L/Bdr	Li Kwok Yan	4863	Pte	Minoot A
4272	Gnr	Li Lai On	4079	Pte	Neves J M
	Spr	Li Ming	4357	Gnr	Ng Chik Hong
	Spr	Li Ping Shum	2621	Gnr	Ng G Kau Tim
	Spr	Li Ping Tsan	5193	Gnr	Ng H A

Did Not Enter POW Camps or Escaped in Early 1942

No	Rank	Name	No	Rank	Name
3433	Gnr	Ng Hang On		Gnr	Shaw C
	Pte	Ng Pak Chuen	4179	Pte	Shi M
	Cpl	Ng Wing		Capt	Shore L R
5081	Pte	Ng Yin Po	2340	Pte	Silva F H
	Spr	Ngan Chung Hon		Lieut	Silva H J
4748	Pte	Ngan Poon Lap	4806	Pte	Sim S
4834	Pte	Oh Bak Chua	2490	L/Cpl	Singh Jiwan
2873	Pte	Olaes J R	4984	Gnr	Siu R
4998	Spr	Ollsson A N	3382	Spr	Smirnoff G V
	Pte	Ooi Seng Poy	2899	L/Cpl	So Yan Kit
5263	Pte	Ou Siew Leng		Pte	Souza L V J de
3505	Gnr	Pang Oi Ling		Pte	Souza V F
3116	Pte	Pang Shiu Wah	2482	Pte	Sprinkle W A
3015	Pte	Pang Yu Tong	4300	Gnr	Sum Chan Chip
3483	L/Bdr	Pao Ching Wah	3239	Pte	Tam Cheong Kee
2929	Spr	Pao Yue Lum	3424	Gnr	Tam Hok Nin
3566	Pte	Passos E F		Spr	Tam Kwan
4396	Pte	Penn Yeuk Wing	4749	Pte	Tam Kwong Lam
3567	Pte	Pereira A A		Pte	Tam P T
	Spr	Ping Kwai	5163	Gnr	Tam Suen Keng
4105	Gnr	Poon Fook Ming		Cpl	Tam Sung Kit
4649	Pte	Pow Tat Lun		Spr	Tam Tak Leung
2563	Cpl	Poy W G	4397	Pte	Tam W
	Sgt	Pun Chi Fan	3070	Bdr	Tam Yan Kwong
	Spr	Pun Heung	5040	Pte	Tan Bieuw
3117	L/Cpl	Pun Iu Chiu	4807	Pte	Tan Luen Hooi
DR 44	Gnr	Rainey J	2951	Sgm	Tan S B
3320	Pte	Reis A D	3122	Pte	Tang Chu
3166	Pte	Remedios A A	2620	L/S	Tang H Yew Hung
3640	Fte	Remedios H A R	3475	Gnr	Tang King Man
3079	Pte	Remedios L M	3118	Pte	Tang Ming Wah
4528	Pte	Ribeiro A J V	2806	L/Cpl	Tang Tung Hoi
2358	Pte	Ribeiro V A V	2623	Gnr	Tang W Yew Ming
3620	Pte	Ribeiro V A V	4809	Pte	Tarn Hock San
3678	L/Cpl	Rocha L A	2588	L/Cpl	Tavares A A
2593	Bdr	Rocha L L	3578	Pte	Tavares E J
3699	Pte	Rosario C M	2782	Pte	Tavares F M
3697	Pte	Rosario J M	3579	Pte	Tavares M A
3571	Pte	Rosario L A	2752	Sgm	Tcheng Pao King
	Spr	Roza A B da	4758	Pte	Teoh Tiaw Bee
	Spr	Roza L A da	DR 22	Pte	Thom W
4543	L/Cpl	Rumjahn A M	4311	Pte	Thomas H
4083	Pte	Santos F A	4759	Pte	Thum Kim Wai
1944	Pte	Santos J A	4736	Pte	Ting Ping Kwan
3700	Pte	Sequeira F X		Spr	To King Shun
3189	CMO	Shapiro E	4819	Pte	Tong Kwok Kee

Did Not Enter POW Camps or Escaped in Early 1942

No	Rank	Name	No	Rank	Name
3099	L/Cpl	Tsang For Pui	2618	Sgm	Wong Q
3095	Pte	Tsang Pang Fei	3096	Pte	Wong Shui Kwong
4673	Pte	Tsang Pong	2902	Pte	Wong Sui Kan
3447	Gnr	Tsang Shiu Woon	3244	Pte	Wong Yin Shau
	Pte	Tsang Yeung	3254	Pte	Wong Yuk Tong
3008	L/Cpl	Tse Kwing In	4539	Gnr	Woo P Tak Ming
2660	Gnr	Tse L	3270	Pte	Woo S Y
4749	Pte	Tseung Ying Hung	DR122	Pte	Woodier J H
3006	Pte	Tso Kwok Fai		Gnr	Wu T C
4151	Gnr	Tso M Him Chi	3392	Pte	Xavier A G
4404	Pte	Tso Wai Huen	3058	L/Cpl	Yee D W
3022	Pte	Tsui Shu Hung	2960	Sgm	Yee J R
3541	Sgt	Turner H	4563	L/Bdr	Yee Man Sum
	Pte	Tweedie J T	2863	Pte	Yeung Chan Fan
3859	Cpl	Ushakoff G E		Spr	Yeung Kin Yau
	Pte	Venpin J	4274	Gnr	Yeung Koon Yuk
4303	Gnr	Wan J		Pte	Yeung Man Ting
3656	Pte	Way W K	2854	L/S	Yeung Man Yeuk
DR 24	Pte	Wilkinson RJ	4761	Pte	Yeung Ming Hon
4812	L/Cpl	Wong Chin Wah	4712	Pte	Yeung Wah Sang
4679	Pte	Wong Cho Yau	3479	Gnr	Yeung Yuk Wah
3429	Gnr	Wong F T	3140	Sgm	Yip Bink K
2711	Pte	Wong H		Pte	Yong P P F
2912	Pte	Wong H S	4275	Gnr	Young C
4739	Pte	Wong Hok	2867	Cpl	Young K O
3274	Pte	Wong Hop Yu	4425	Pte	Young W R
4676	Pte	Wong J	3127	L/S	Yu Fook Sang
3252	L/Cpl	Wong K P	4817	Pte	Yu Shiu On
2997	L/Cpl	Wong Kam Fu		Gnr	Yuen H
4760	Pte	Wong Ki Lun	3226	Spr	Yuen S L
	Pte	Wong Kok Fui	3451	L/Bdr	Yung Fook Hoi
	Spr	Wong Kong	4155	L/Bdr	Yung J
	Spr	Wong Ming Hin	4367	Gnr	Yung Kam Ling
4677	Pte	Wong Mun	4843	Pte	Yvanovich V A Jr,
5038	Pte	Wong Ngai Mun	2855	Bdr	Zaman M J
2823	Pte	Wong P		Gnr	Zie Yuen

Movements after the Surrender Uncertain

No	Rank	Name	No	Rank	Name
	Pte	Adam M		L/Cpl	Leung T H
B544		Akbar K		L/Cpl	Lew K S
	Cpl	Bond			Lim H
	Pte	Bonnen J R			Ling C S
	Cpl	Britton J	4177		Lo P W
	Pte	Chak P T		Pte	Lum D
	Dvr	Chan M F		Pte	Lum P
	Pte	Chan T K			Mok K K
	Gnr	Chan Y K		Capt	Moran J
	Pte	Cheong A		Spr	Morgan E F A
2619	Sgt	Coppin A		Cpl	Murray J A
	Cpl	Fidler		Gnr	Ng W S
	Pte	Geoghan "Paddy"			Noble H
	2/Lieut	Gordon C			Parkes B
		Gosano L		Lieut	Philip D G
		Gosano Z		Pte	Tan H S
742	Pte	Graves W		Cpl	Tang W B
		Greenheld		Pte	Tong S M
	Pte	Guy A L		L/Cpl	Wan S H
	Spr	Jeffreys J			Wilmer H B
	Pte	Kuz J V Da			Wong C P
	Gnr	Kwok L J		Cpl	Wong P C
	Cpl	Lau S L		L/Sgt	Xavier J M
	L/Cpl	Laurie J			Yip C
	Pte	Lee F			Zeferino L

Killed in Action or Died of Wounds

No	Rank	Name		No	Rank	Name	
DR 234	Gnr	Alexander W L	K 24	1708	Sgt	Brown H W	K 17
3366	Pte	Alves H A	U 19	2749	L/Bdr	Buckingham A W	U 25
	Lieut	Anderson D J N	K 19		L/Cpl	Burson H	K 21
	Pte	Andrews A	U 19	3481	Gnr	Butlin S T	K 25
DR 111	Pte	Andrews H H	U 19		Lieut	Buxton H T	K 18
	Sgt	Bagley W G	U 25		Pte	Calman A	U 23
4571	Gnr	Bakar A	K 18	4836	Gnr	Campos H M	K 18
3834	Sgt	Bannister E W	U 18		Pte	Carr G	U 24
DR 128	Pte	Barton W M	K 23	4134	Gnr	Chan U Chan	K 18
	Pte	Blackman D	K 24	3030	Pte	Cheng K S	K 25
4246	Gnr	Bliss A S	K 25	4840	Gnr	Cheung Wing Yee	K 18
3224	Sgt	Bone A	K 24		Pte	Chung Yew Mun	U 19
	Cpl	Bonner H W	K 22	3113	L/Bdr	Collins-Taylor D	HU25
2235	Gnr	Broadbridge W E	K 18		Pte	Coull D	K 24
	Pte	Brown C	U 22		Pte	Cox C W	U 19

Killed in Action or Died of Wounds

No	Rank	Name	
	Pte	Crossan J	U 24
	Pte	Cullen W F	U 20
	Cpl	Cunningham A L	K 23
2104	Sgt	Curtis E L	U 19
	CQMS	Cuthill G H	U 21
	Pte	Delcourt A	U 21
	Pte	Des Voeux Sir E	U 19
DR 145	L/Cpl	Drummond A	
5164	Gnr	Duffy J T	U 25
	Pte	Edwards P	U 19
	2/Lieut	Edwards R	K 21
	Pte	Egan R J	K 21
	Pte	Elliott F	U 22
PG 223	Pte	Fateh Mohamed	K 25
3791	BQMS	Fernandez I M	U 15
4225	Bdr	Fincher E F	K 18
	L/Cpl	Fisher E D	K 19
4357	Gnr	Floisand A	K 25
	Pte	Ford W F	U 24
	Major	Forsyth H R	K 24
	Pte	Fox G E	U 22
	Pte	Fox O	K 19
4172	Gnr	France N H	K 20
	Cpl	Gaubert E	U 25
3348	Gnr	Gerzo S D	K 25
	Pte	Gill J	K 24
	Pte	Gillies H O	
			U 5.1.42 (3.1.42)
4417	Pte	Goldman R	U 19
	Pte	Gosling R G	U 19
	Pte	Gowland C M	U 24
	Pte	Grant I F	K 25
4089	Gnr	Greaves S E	K 18
1641	Gnr	Griffiths R H	K 25
	Pte	Hall S W	K 19
	Pte	Hardwick D W	U 26
	Pte	Hearne H J A	K 25
	Sgt	Hillier W S	K 22
	Cpl	Hing E	U 19
4239	Gnr	Ho A	K 18
	Pte	Ho A L	U 19
5169	Gnr	Ho L K	U 25
	Pte	Hobbs B C	U 25
	Pte	Hoffman J J	K 19
	Capt	Holmes L B	K 19
	Pte	Hone A	U 19

No	Rank	Name	
	Pte	Hoselitz R	U 21
	Cpl	Houghton J M	U 21
3237	Pte	Hryniewicz V	U 19
3652	Pte	Humphrey P H	U 19
	L/Cpl	Hung Kai Chiu	K 19
5002	Spr	Hyndman E	K 31
	Pte	Izatt S B	K 19
	Capt	Jacoste F M	U 19
	L/Cpl	Jessop J E	U 19
	Pte	Jitts G C	K 19
	Pte	Job A E	U 19
	Gnr	Johnson L G	U 25
	2/Lieut	Jones H S	K 25
	Pte	Jorge F J	U 22
	Pte	Joseph H B	U 22
	Pte	Kerbey G H	U 24
	Pte	Kern E	U 22
4716	Pte	Kjaer K S	U 19
4301	Gnr	Kossakowsky F A	K 25
4317	Gnr	Kwok Wing Ching	K 18
	CQMS	Lacey J T	K 24
	Pte	Lambert W R	U 25
4864	Gnr	Lander J G H	K 25
4505	L/Bdr	Lao Hsin Nain	K 18
	Pte	Lau George	U 19
	Pte	Lau T S	U 19
4800	Gnr	Lawson W G	K 25
3245	L/Cpl	Leung Chik Wai	K 25
4186	Gnr	Leung Fook Wing	K 18
	Pte	Leung T C	U 19
	Pte	Lim A	U 19
4343	Gnr	Lim J A	U 25
	Pte	Lim J P F	U 19
	L/Cpl	Lim Kim Huan	U 19
	Pte	Lim S T	U 19
3403	Gnr	Lipkovsky B	U 25
DR 63	Gnr	Litton J L	K 18
4666	Pte	Lo W C	U 19
3379	Gnr	Lodge C J	U 25
	Pte	Lowry G T	U 25
	Pte	Lyen E S	U 22
DR 151	Gnr	Lyon D	K 25
	Pte	MacKay C H	U 25
	Pte	MacKechnie G M	U 19
	P/Major	MacKie W C K	U 24
	Pte	Maher A P	U 19

Killed in Action or Died of Wounds

No	Rank	Name	
	CQMS	Mann A	U 22
	Pte	Markham W	U 19
2831	L/Cpl	Marques C A	U 19
DR 95	Pte	Martin F	K 30.1.42
3176	Pte	Maxwell R D	K 23
DR 182	Gnr	McCabe L H	U 25
4164	Sgt	McCallum D	U 22
	Pte	McCormick C J C	K 24
	Pte	McLeod A	U 24
1964	Sgt	Millington H J	K 25
	Pte	Minhinett J D	U 22
DR 312	Pte	Mogra J E	K 4.1.42
	Pte	Muir A W	U 19
	2/Lieut	Muir H G	K 25
	Pte	Murphy J	U 24
4997	Gnr	Nash R C	K 25
	Pte	Newhouse G	U 24
3040	Cpl	Ng Po Lau	K 25
3357	Pte	Noronha F A	U 18
1990	Bdr	Orr D	K 25
4198	Gnr	Ozorio M H	K 18
	Pte	Park W	U 19
4861	Gnr	Paterson E M	K 18
	Pte	Pearce T E	U 19
	Pte	Pearce T H	U 24
	Pte	Peters W H	U 22
	CQMS	Polson J C	
			K 2.1.42 (14.1.42)
4188	Gnr	Poon Kwong Kuen	K 18
4372	Pte	Pospisil A	U 24
	CSM	Potter J E	U 25
	Pte	Prew A G F	U 22
	Pte	Rapp F A	U 22
	Pte	Rathsam H W	U 22
	Pte	Reed A A	U 19
	Pte	Reed E V	U 19
2798	Gnr	Reed F O	K 18
3856	Pte	Reed S A	K 15.1.42
4538	L/Bdr	Rocha A J	U 18
	Pte	Rodgers R A	U 19
DR 52	L/Bdr	Rouban M J	K 22
4415	Gnr	Rudrof W P	K 25
2200	Gnr	Samuel H A	K 25
3349	Gnr	Sayers M W	K 25

No	Rank	Name	
4217	L/Bdr	Schnepel F	K 15
3325	Pte	Sequeira L R	K 15
PG 95	Pte	Shah Ghulam Hossain	
			K 25
	L/Cpl	Sharp W	U 23
	Pte	Sim J	U 19
	Sgt	Skinner L D	U 21
4326	Gnr	Smith C A	K 25
3411	Gnr	Smith J R M	K 24
	Pte	Smits H W	U 19
	Pte	Sorby V	
			K 16.1.42 (15.1.42)
5171	Gnr	Stafford A B	K 25
3353	Cpl	Stephens J L	U 11
	Sgt	Stephens J R	K 21
4798	Gnr	Stokes G D	K 18
3227	L/Bdr	Stone G P	K 25
DR 9	Gnr	Stone W E	K 18
	CSM	Swan T	K 24
	L/Cpl	Thom C S M	U 25
4304	L/Bdr	Thomerson G	U 25
	Pte	Thomson J M	K 24
4198	Gnr	Tsang Ka Pen	K 18
5172	Gnr	Tse Wai Man	U 21
4615	Gnr	Ulrich A	K 18
DR 72	Gnr	Ulrich P H A	K 18
4573	Pte	Van Leeuwen H	K 19
3716	Pte	Walker J M	U 19
	Pte	Watson K	K 24
DH 215	L/Cpl	White N B	U 22
3104	Sgt	White N L	K 22
4685	Gnr	Wilkens K	U 25
DR 31	Gnr	Wilkinson J N	K 18
	L/Cpl	Williams C L	U 25
3389	Bdr	Wilson P B	U 19
2869	Pte	Wong S H	U 29
	Pte	Wylie L M	U 19
DR 165	Gnr	Wyllie R L	K 25
	Pte	Young E B	U 19
	L/Cpl	Young W	U 19
4222	Gnr	Yung Yue Wang	U 25
	Pte	Zaharoff V I	U 22
	Sgt	Zimmern	U 19
4268	L/Bdr	Zimmern A	K 18

Died whilst Prisoners of War

No	Rank	Name	Date of Death	Cemetery
2841	Pte	Ainslie G	K 20.8.42	
	Pte	Angus G I	K 29.1.45	Yokohama
3542	Gnr	Baker L C	K 12.8.42	
	Pte	Baladin G (alias Bel)	K 3.11.44	Yokohama
2437	Pte	Barros L A	K 23.8.43	HKRCC
1923	CSM	Baskett P E	K 9.12.43	
4989	Pte	Benjamin V	U 21.9.45	Died soon after Release
	2/Lieut	Bowker A C I	K 2.10.42	
1290	CSM	Britto H M	K 31.1.43	
4052	Pte	Brown W J	K 14.5.43	
	Pte	Buchanan G	K 25.10.42	
2965	Cpl	Budden G E	K 11.10.42	
4995	Pte	Buis J G	15.11.44	
2795	Pte	Cave L J	K 16.11.42	
4354	L/Bdr	Christensen N O	K 18.12.42	
	Pte	Cross G E	K 10.12.42	
64	Cpl	Cullen F	K 2.3.45	
4856	Gnr	Dodwell M C	K 15.5.44	
3736	Cpl	Doxford W	U 10.9.45	Died soon after Release
3192	Cpl	Elliott W	K 30.6.44	
DR 162	L/Cpl	Farmer C L	K 7.10.43	
3181	Gnr	Ferguson J S	K 25.11.42	
3586	Pte	Fernandes E A	K 18.12.44	Yokohama
4830	Sgm	Fleming W	K 5.12.44	Yokohama
421	Pte	Forsyth W R	K 23.11.43	
	Cpl	Foster G B	K 8.7.44	
2477	Pte	Franco E M	K 29.1.45	Yokohama
4664	Gnr	Gaunt J A	K 4.1.44	
3161	Sgt	Gittins W M	K 5.3.45	Yokohama
3375	Sgt	Gow D	K 12.4.44	Yokohama
	Lieut	Guterres J J	K 26.7.42	
	Pte	Hailey G	K 24.7.42	
DR 319	Spr	Hale F M	K 26.8.44	
3293	Pte	Harrington G T	K 14.8.42	
2141	L/Cpl	Hickman J P	K 26.9.42	
3111	Bdr	Higgins J J	K 21.2.43	
3893	L/Cpl	Hill R A	K 27.9.44	Yokohama
DR 294	Cpl	Hood J M	K 21.3.44	Yokohama
3051	Gnr	Houston T J	K 4.12.42	
1835	Sgt	Hunt H J	K 31.5.44	
209	WO 1	Jack J M	K 15.9.44	Yokohama
1834	Sgt	Jack L	K 22.8.42	
1971	Sgm	Johnson I G	K 5.4.42	
4643	Cpl	Lacey H	K 21.5.42	
DR 88	Pte	Lawrence J H	K 29.5.42	CCRCC
4667	L/Cpl	Lee J S	K 1.10.44	Yokohama

Died whilst Prisoners of War

No	Rank	Name	Date of Death	Cemetery
2969	Sgt	Lloyd N D	K 25.4.42	
	Pte	Longfield S	K 18.8.42	
4645	L/Cpl	MacKinnon J M	K 28.11.44	Yokohama
	Spr	Marriott H	K 14.2.42	
4661	Gnr	Mathieu P B N	K 27.8.43	
2714	L/Cpl	Mendonca M	U Date unknown	
3288	Pte	Moore D R H	K 30.4.42	
DR 144	Pte	Morphew P L	K 29.10.42	
	Pte	Murray I N	K 1.6.43 (31.5.43)	
DR 203	L/Cpl	Pragnell C F	K 12.9.42	
3606	Pte	Prata M G	K 14.9.43	HKRCC - BAAG Executed
	Pte	Rapp F C	K 12.8.42	
2231	CSM	Rathmell R	K 26.10.42	
4059	Pte	Ribeiro E A V	K 23.8.42	
4420	Pte	Roberts S E	K 16.8.42	
3771	L/Sgt	Ryan P	K 14.5.43	
	Lieut	Shrigley R J	K 28.6.44	
4051	Cpl	Shuster E	K 1.3.44	Yokohama
3615	Pte	Silva A C	K 8.7.45	
	Capt	Smith S G	K 20.7.44	
2440	Pte	Soares A C	K 3.1.44	
	Pte	Stanesby S J C	K 14.5.42	
3075	Cpl	Stimpson C C	K 27.8.43	
1454	L/Cpl	Sturgeon J B	K 2.1.42	
3793	Bdr	Tansley W A	K 2.4.45	
2354	L/Cpl	Thompson W J	K 9.4.42	
2691	BSM	Walker W L	K 3.3.44	Yokohama
3688	Gnr	Weill L	K 27.4.44	HKJC
3874	Sgt	Whittaker W H	K 7.12.43	HKC
3898	Sgt	Woolley W J	K 25.3.44	

Transferred to Other Units on Outbreak of Hostilities

No	Rank	Name	Transferred to	Date	Remarks
	2/Lieut	Andrews L R	R A	8 Dec 41	
	Lt Col	Black G D R	R A M C (Lt)	8 Dec 41	K Dec 25
3888	L/Cpl	Clark J L	E Service	8 Dec 41	
	2/Lieut	Elliott F A M	R A	8 Dec 41	
	Pte	Gilmore W C G	2/14 Punjab R (2/Lt)	14 Dec 41	K 9.4.42
	Cpl	Gordon V R	R Scots (2/Lt)	17 Dec 41	K 6.1.42
	2/Lieut	Guinness A H	R A	8 Dec 41	
	Pte	Hamilton G C	R Scots (2/Lt)	17 Dec 41	
	2/Lieut	Hobbin W R	R A	8 Dec 41	
4828	Pte	Kerr I A F	HQ C C (2/Lt)	24 Dec 41	
	Pte	Lammert L E	5/7 Rajput R (2/Lt)	14 Dec 41	U Dec 19
	Sgt	Lawrie J F	Gen List / R A (2/Lt)	8 Dec 41	U Dec 19
	Sgt	MacKenzie A K	R Scots (2/Lt)	17 Dec 41	
	2/Lieut	MacKinlay W A	Mx Regt	8 Dec 41	K Dec 24
	L/Cp1	Matthews E A	5/7 Rajput R (2/Lt)	14 Dec 41	U Dec 18
	Lt Col	Owen-Hughes, H.	LO in Chungking	9 Dec 41	
4765	Spr	Perkins V A	E Service	14 Dec 41	
	Pte	Swettenham G F	R Scots (2/Lt)	17 Dec 41	U Dec 19
	2/Lieut	Turner N H	R A	8 Dec 41	
	2/Lieut	Walkden A F	R A	8 Dec 41	
	2/Lieut	Whitham J P	Mx Regt	8 Dec 41	U 1.10.42 Lisbon Maru
3900	Spr	Young J	E Services	8 Dec 41	
3533	Spr	Yow W	A T S	8 Dec 41	

Fought with the HKVDC until the Surrender and then Joined Other Units

No	Rank	Name	Transferred to	Remarks
3236	Sgt	Bosanquet D I	R A	Escaped from POW Camp
	Pte	Chan King	BAAG	Did not enter POW Camp Died - Unconfirmed
	Sgt	Farrell R E		
4820	Pte	Ho B	BAAG	Did not enter POW Camp
	L/Cpl	Holmes D R	Ind Army / BAAG	Escaped Capture
2845	Pte	Hung A	Ind Army / BAAG	
	L/Cpl	Hung D	Ind Army / BAAG	
		Ip M M	BAAG	
	Pte	Kotwall G	BAAG	Did not enter POW Camp Executed K 29.10.43
4675	Pte	Lam D	BAAG	Released from POW Camp
2722	L/Cpl	Lee Yiu Piu	Ind Army / BAAG	Escaped from POW Camp
2914	Sgt	Lo Hung Sui	BAAG	Did not enter POW Camp
	Pte	McEwan C M	Gen List / BAAG	Escaped Capture
2923	Sgt	Mok Wah Chan	BAAG	Released from POW Camp
770	Pte	Monaghan T C	BAAG	Did not enter POW Camp Executed K 29.10.43
2367	Cpl	Quah F E Cheow	BAAG	Did not enter POW Camp
	Lt Col	Ride L T	Ind Army / BAAG	Escaped from POW Camp
	CQMS	Stott R E	Ind Army	Escaped
	Pte	Talan M	Gen List/ Force 136	Escaped Capture
	2/Lieut	Teesdale E B	Ind Army / Force 136 / BAAG	Escaped Capture
	CMO	Thomas O	Gen List / Force 136 / BAAG	Escaped Capture
	Capt	Trevor I B	Imp Forces	Escaped from POW Camp
	Pte	Zimmern W A	Ind Army / BAAG	

Did not enter POW Camp and joined the BAAG "China Unit"

Subsequently transferred to the Chindits in Burma. Full list is unknown.

No	Rank	Name	No	Rank	Name
4616	Gnr	Cheng Maximo	3796	Gnr	Reeves J W
4871	Cpl	Fox L A	4686	Gnr	So Tse Yiu
3432	Gnr	Ho Sang	4385	Gnr	Tai Robert
4659	Gnr	Liu Tam Choi	4549	Gnr	Tsang K M George
3784		Ozorio A M (Ozorio F A)	5167	Gnr	Wong Johnny
DR 204		Quie J L			

Did not Mobilise

No	Rank	Name	No	Rank	Name
	Gnr	Adams W B			MacIndoe A
DR 131	Pte	Agafuroff I			Mak Shun Ming
	Pte	Alves A G V		L/Bdr	Melrose W
	Pte	Alves AJ		Gnr	Ng C H
3319	Pte	Antonio P E	1495	Pte	Oliveira J M
2448	Pte	Baptista C O		Pte	Oliveira M A
	Gnr	Bau K K	3138	Pte	Ozorio A M
	Gnr	Bovaird W C	DR 197	Gnr	Pattinson F K
3004	Sgt	Cash A I		Pte	Prata F A
3090	Pte	Chan K O		Pte	Remedios C H V
	Pte	Chan M C	2450	Pte	Rocha J G da
	Gnr	Cheng Wat	3151	Pte	Roza L M da
	Pte	Chow J	4108	L/Cpl	Rumianzeff V D
Deceased		Dessoulavy M M	3527	L/Cpl	Sing T
	Gnr	Doo W	3617	Pte	Souza A M P
	Pte	Guterres A M	3618	Pte	Souza M G P
	Cpl	Hammond V M		L/Bdr	Streatfield E P
	Gnr	Heung Hock Chau		L/Cpl	Tam H T
2012	Pte	Hansen W J			Tam Wai Sun
	Gnr	Houghton M F		BSM	Thomas F L
	Gnr	Hui Koon Fat			Thompson G B S
DR59	Gnr	Kitchell A	4795	Gnr	Tsang Chor Kwan
	Pte	Lam K F		Gnr	Tso Chi
4393	Pte	Lau Wing Cho		Gnr	Treskin V
3092	Pte	Lee Shui Ping		Gnr	Watson J A
3434	Gnr	Lee W C		Gnr	Willey F J
	Pte	Leung C Y	1959	Cpl	Willis D J
	Spr	Leung Fan		L/Cpl	Wolfe J
	Gnr	Leung Kui So	3248	Pte	Wong Sui In
		Leung On Kwok	2431	Pte	Xavier A E
	Pte	Lindblom G L	2853	Pte	Yeung C F
DR 118	Gnr	Low W C		Pte	Yim Y
	Pte	Luz L A D	3030	Pte	Yuen C L

Nursing Detachment

No	Name	Remarks	No	Name	Remarks
68	Andrews-Loving I		145	Hills E A	Sister
2	Baldwin P G		51	Hillier N	
149	Beaman M	Sister	58	Hobbs R E	Sister
7	Beaumont V		57	Hogg E F	Sister
12	Beavis E M		61	Judah R	
10	Begdon D M		62	Judah R R	
17	Begg E	K 25	63	Kelvin-Stark D	
11	Berruex M		27	Kennard D M	
71	Bidwell E J		67	Leghorn H K	Sister
14	Black A J		64	Lloyd J G	
6	Black A		66	Longbottom B E	
3	Booker D		70	Longbottom D	
5	Booke		142	Lovzevitch E	
1	Braude I M S	Commanding	143	Lowe E M	
139	Buckle M	Sister	84	Mabb R S	
8	Budden M		72	Mace P H	
16	Burnie C P		75	Mackinlay S M	
15	Butlin E	Sister	76	Macleod W M	
9	Buxton A	K 25	77	McGuffog M S	
15	Carruthers M D		74	Matthews M G	
25	Carter B C		48	Millar R	
20	Cassidy M J	Assistant Com'd	99	Mills B de C M	
22	Cautherley D A		150	Morosov L	
94	Challinor J S		80	Muir A S	
79	Channing M		131	Needham F P	Sister
23	Church B V		85	Newnham P E	
21	Colledge P R		96	Peers C M	
26	Crawhall-Wilson H		125	Pennington G A	
60	Crofton G T		89	Philippens E M	
29	Drummond M M	Sister	91	Poltock P T	
33	Ellis G		95	Potter L	
32	Ellis L	K 17.8.42	90	Pritchard E E	
31	Ellis S		97	Quin N	
35	Fidoe E A	Sister	102	Raymond R	
39	Flippance A L	Sister	151	Redwood M	
146	Gehring C		152	Reeves R	
147	Gehring R		98	Richards M A	
46	Godfrey C	Sister	105	Richardson E C	
42	Grady A M		104	Ritchie I C	
49	Graham-Barrow J		148	Robson C M	Sister
135	Gray E F		101	Ross G R	
44	Gray E M		106	Rudolf M M	Sister
40	Greaves A	Sister	107	Sanh C M	
45	Groundwater J		111	Sanh J C	
47	Gubbay S	K 17.5.42 HKJC	112	Sanh M K	
56	Hill B I		117	Scotcher P	

Nursing Detachment

No	Name	Remarks	No	Name	Remarks
115	Seath E		121	Thom A	
116	Shore C	Sister	140	Tonoff E	
109	Simmons G G		127	Wallace M M M	
108	Simpson A V F		82	Weilandt J M T	
138	Sinclair G M M		129	White G F	
118	Smith M M	K 25		White V	Quartermaster
119	Spradberry B		128	Whittaker W W	
153	Stoneman K		93	Willoughby E M	
136	Stoneman M P		122	Witchell V M	
114	Sutton W M		110	Wood I J	
120	Tebbutt E A				

PWD Corps

Under the Civil Defence Corps Regulations of July 1941, auxiliary organisations were formed for the performance of essential services. The Public Works Corps, the PWD Corps, was included in October 1941. Members of that Corps who were members of the HKVDC remained as members of the HKVDC.

No	Rank	Name	Initial Internment	Remarks
3228	Sgt	Bailey J D	Stanley	HKVDC until 16 Dec 41
	QMS	Beach		
	S/Sgt	Bell R S		K 26 Dec 41
	WOI	Bolt	Stanley	
	Lieut	Brown J C	Stanley	
	Lieut	Clarke A E	Stanley	
	Major	Cryan R	Stanley	
	S/Sgt	Davidson D		Death Unconfirmed 22 Dec 41
	WOI	Ewing	Stanley	
	S/Sgt	Flegg J S		K 22 Dec 41
4092	Spr	George S W		HKVDC until 16 Dec 41
	WOI	Griggs G W R	Stanley	
	S/Sgt	Howard A H	POW	
	Sgt	Jeavons G F	POW	
	WO II	May A F	House Arrest	Interned in Mau Tau Chung from August 44
	Lieut	Owen W H	Stanley	HKVDC until 8 Dec 41
	CSM	Shaw W	Stanley	U 9.May.42
	Capt	White S O		
	Sgt	Woolgar G D	POW	

The above list may contain some who were not mobilised in December 1941. Those listed are not included elsewere in the Nominal Roll of the Hong Kong Volunteer Defence Corps.

APPENDIX V

Honours and Awards Received

Resulting from the Defence of Hong Kong, the subsequent internment as Prisoners of War, escapes from captivity and subsequent actions in the war in South-East Asia a number of members of the Hong Kong Volunteer Defence Corps received Awards or were Mentioned.

Awards Received in Recognition of Gallant and Distinguished Services

Commander of the Most Excellent Order of the British Empire (CBE)

Services in the field
Col L. T. Ride OBE   9 November 1944
(As an Indian Army Officer)

Officer of the Most Excellent Order of the British Empire (OBE)

Services in the field
Lt Col L. T. Ride   16 June 1942

Distinguished Service Order (DSO)

Services in the Defence of Hong Kong in December 1941
Maj E. G. Stewart   4 April 1946

Member of the Most Excellent Order of the British Empire (MBE)

Services in the field

Capt D R Holmes MC   4 May 1943

Maj C. M. McEwan   15 November 1945
(As an Officer on the General List)

Capt Lee Yiu-piu MM   18 April 1946
(As an Indian Army Officer)

Maj M. Talan   6 June 1946
(As an Officer on the General List)

Services in the Defence of Hong Kong in December 1941
Capt D. L. Strellett   4 April 1946

Services whilst engaged in Special Operations in South East Asia
Lt O. Thomas   7 November 1946
(As an Officer on the General List)

Honours and Awards Received

Military Cross (MC)
Services in the field
Capt D R Holmes	9 March 1943
Capt I. B. Trevor	18 August 1942

Services in the Defence of Hong Kong in December 1941
Lt B. C. Field	4 April 1946
Lt I. P. Tamworth	4 April 1946
2/Lt M. G. Carruthers	4 April 1946

Services whilst engaged in Special Operations in South East Asia
Maj E. B. Teesdale	7 November 1946
(As an Officer in the Indian Army)	

Distinguished Conduct Medal (DCM)
Services in the Defence of Hong Kong in December 1941
Sgt T. F. Stainton	4 April 1946

Military Medal (MM)
Services in the field
Sgt Lee Yiu-piu	16 June 1946
Sgt D. I. Bosanquet	7 January 1943

Services in the Defence of Hong Kong in December 1941
Sgt H. V. Pearse	4 April 1946
Sgt C. D. Walker	4 April 1946
L/Cpl W. D. Yee	4 April 1946
Sgm C. L Salter	4 April 1946
Cpl W. G. Poy	29 August 1946
CSM V. White	29 August 1946

British Empire Medal (BEM)
For special services during the enemy occupation of Hong Kong
Student David Lam	21 January 1947

For services in the Field, prior to September 1945
L/Sgt D. J. Leonard	26 June 1947

Honours and Awards Received

Mentioned in recognition of gallant and distinguished service

Services in the Defence of Hong Kong in December 1941

Maj H. R. Forsyth (killed in action)	28 February 1946
Maj J. J. Patterson	4 April 1946
Sister E. A. Hills	4 April 1946
WOII A. T. Begg	4 April 1946
Sgt N. J. Booker	4 April 1946
Sgt T. Davis	4 April 1946
Sgt D. Gow (posthumous)	4 April 1946
Cpl W. Elliott (posthumous)	4 April 1946
L/Cpl W. Eu	4 April 1946
L/Cpl K. C. Hung (posthumous)	4 April 1946
L/Bdr Li Kwok-yan	4 April 1946
Pte G. A. White	4 April 1946
Pte G. C. Jitts (posthumous)	4 April 1946
Sgt G. Winch	29 August 1946

Services in the field

Capt K. Valentine	29 August 1946
Lt D. L. Prophet	29 August 1946
Pte M. G. Prata (posthumous)	29 August 1946
Capt R. Egal	21 January 1947

Services while Prisoners of War

Capt R. R. Davies	12 September 1946
Lt K. M. A. Barnett	12 September 1946

Other Awards Received

Officer of the Most Excellent Order of the British Empire (OBE)

Lt Col H. Owen Hughes	10 June 1948

Member of the Most Excellent Order of the British Empire (MBE)

Sgt Maj F C Jones	1 January 1947
WOII M. N. Rakusen	1 January 1948
Capt A. M. Rodrigues	10 June 1948
CSM M. F. de P. Baptista	1 January 1949
Capt H. A. de B. Botelho	9 June 1949

Honours and Awards Received

Many of those members of the HKVDC in December 1941 went on to serve in the successor units. The following subsequently received military awards for their service.

Officer of the Most Excellent Order of the British Empire (OBE)

Maj E. G. Stewart DSO	1 January 1955
Col H. A. de B. Botelho MBE	1 January 1967

Member of the Most Excellent Order of the British Empire (MBE)

Maj A. N. Braude	1 June 1953
Maj G. H. Calvert	1 January 1954
Lt E. C. Fincher	1 January 1954
Maj B. C. Field MC	10 June 1954
Capt F. V. V. Ribeiro	10 June 1954
Maj R. S. Capell	10 June 1961
Maj S. M. Bard	1 January 1968
Maj G. E. K. Roylance	12 June 1971

British Empire Medal

Cpl N. C. Barretto	1 January 1957.

The dates are as included in the Supplement to The London Gazette and the ranks are those held at the time of the award. It is appreciated that the list may not be complete but no other record is known to exist. Any omission is regretted.

APPENDIX VI

About the Author

COLONEL Evan George STEWART DSO, OBE, ED, MA

Born on 27 March 1892 in Bedford, the seventh child of the Rev Robert Warren Stewart MA and Louisa (nee Smyly), both CMS missionaries in China who were then on home leave.

He went with his parents to their mission station in Kucheng, Fukien Province, East China, in 1893 and was with them in 1895 at a nearby hill station called Hwa-sang when they were attacked by an insurgent group, the so-called "Vegetarians", who were opposed to all foreigners, particularly missionaries.

His parents were killed as were one of his brothers, Herbert (age 6), and one of his sisters, Hilda (age 1), and their nursemaid. Evan survived, although it is said that he was hit on the head by a rifle butt. Rescued from the then burning house by his sister Kathleen (age 11), who also rescued their sister Mildred (aged 13) whose leg had been slashed by a sword. His elder brothers, Arthur, Phillip and James, were at school in England.

The surviving children were taken to Dublin to their grandfather's large house, *Gortleitragh*, in Kingstown (renamed Dun Laoghaire in 1922), where he, with his brothers and sisters, were brought up by their uncles and aunts. Later they were looked after by their Aunt Emily ("Tem") at her home, *Brighton Lodge*, in nearby Monkstown.

Educated in Dublin and then as a boarder at Wellington College where he shone at Mathematics, History and in Athletics winning the English Public Schools 100yds sprint.

On leaving school in 1910, he went to Hong Kong to teach at St. Paul's College where his older brother Arthur was headmaster; this was partly to raise money to attend University. Joined "The Hong Kong Volunteers" in 1910 and was soon commissioned thanks to his officer training in the O.T.C. at Wellington.

In 1913 he returned to Dublin to attend Trinity College as an undergraduate, reading History. In 1915, with the war becoming ever more demanding, he felt compelled to join up before completing his degree course although, as an undergraduate, he was then exempt from military service.

About the Author

He was commissioned immediately and volunteered for a Machine-gun Regiment, The Middlesex. He served in France, was wounded twice and on one occasion returned to Dublin to convalesce. In France, he briefly met his brother James, an Army Padre who was killed in 1916, and later another brother, Phillip, who was a Major in the RAMC. By the end of the war he was a Captain, acting Major, having been "on active service from 1915 to 1919".

After the trauma of trench warfare he did not feel able to resume his degree course immediately so returned to Hong Kong in 1920 to teach again at St Paul's College. However, realising that he would need a degree to be fully acceptable as a teacher, he took an external London University Degree in History, graduating in 1925. In 1926, Trinity College granted him its Degree and the "right to wear the cap and gown of a graduate of the College" because his studies "had been interrupted by military service".

In 1928 he married Dorothy Sarah Lander, daughter of The Rt Rev G H Lander, Bishop of Hong Kong from 1907 to 1920 and a previous headmaster of St. Paul's College. She was the younger sister of Kathleen, wife to he his brother Arthur. They had one son, Robert Michael, born in 1931.

In 1930 he took over as Headmaster of St. Paul's College, in succession to his brother, and remained headmaster, with the break of wartime, until his death.

When the Japanese invaded Hong Kong in 1941 he was a Major, commanding HKVDC No. 3 (Machine-gun) Company, first on Stonecutters Island and later in the Wong Nei Chong Gap area. His actions were to result in an award of the Distinguished Service Order for which the citation noted that the successful evacuation of Stonecutters while under fire was greatly due to his powers of organisation and leadership; while at Wong Nei Chong Gap, although wounded early in the fighting, he continued to command his Company with a total disregard for his own safety and suffering.

After the capture of Wong Nei Chong Gap by the enemy he organised the escape of the six survivors from that area and finally found his own way back alone through the enemy lines. Throughout, his conduct was an example to all of high courage and coolness. During the fighting at Wong Nei Chong Gap, his Company suffered 100% casualties in officers and over 80% in Other Ranks.

Before the start of hostilities, his wife and son had been evacuated to the Philippines and then to Sydney. After the surrender on Christmas Day 1941 he was interned as a prisoner-of-war in the Argyle Street Camp. His wounds could not be properly treated and so, combined with malnutrition, he became severely ill so that on Liberation he was evacuated first to Australia and then to England to Stoke Mandeville Orthopaedic Hospital.

About the Author

He returned to Hong Kong in 1947, despite a 'dropped-foot' resulting from an inadequately treated shrapnel wound in his spine, and reopened St Paul's College, which had been temporarily restarted as a co-educational school by Katie Wu.

He was Chairman of the HK Inter-Schools Sports Committee, Chairman of the HK School Certificate Panel, a member of the HK University Court, a member of St John's Cathedral Council (and a Sidesman at the Cathedral), a member of St John's College Council, on the Government's Appeals Board and was on several other Boards.

He joined the Hong Kong Regiment, the successor unit to the Hong Kong Defence Corps, and in 1950 transferred to the Home Guard taking over command from October 1953 to 1956. He led the Hong Kong Regiment's contingent in the Coronation Procession in London in 1953, chaired the committee on the history of the HKVDC and was awarded the OBE in 1955. He served as Honorary Colonel of the Hong Kong Regiment from March 1958 until his death later that year.

He died on 17 December 1958, when still Headmaster of St Paul's, at the aged of only 66, mainly from the effects of his time as a prisoner-of-war. His very well attended memorial service was in St John's Cathedral on 23 December and his ashes were dispersed in the grounds of St Paul's College, which had played such a large part in his life.

APPENDIX VII

The 1953 Coronation Procession in London

In June 1953 a contingent from the then Volunteer unit, the Royal Hong Kong Defence Force, sent a contingent to take part in the parade which formed part of the coronation of Her Majesty, Queen Elizabeth who had the previous year succeeded to the throne of the United Kingdom.

The contingent was led by Major E. G. Stewart, D.S.O., E.D who commanded No 3 Company of the HKVDC during the Battle for Hong Kong in December 1941, the author of this book. His article on the Coronation Procession in London was first published in the 1953 Volunteer Magazine.

* * *

East Square of the Royal Artillery Barracks at Woolwich presented a curious spectacle on the evening of May 21st 1953. Some 400 men, representative of 34 colonies and dependencies were collected there, and uniforms, and especially headgear, were wondrously varied. Accommodation was taxed, for the Barracks also contained the R.A. Coronation Contingent as well as its normal complement. Hong Kong shared a barrack-room with Fiji, and found pleasant and congenial stable-mates. The Fijians may be, as the broadcasts described them, "the world's finest jungle fighters", though this has been queried, but they are certainly among the world's finest rugby players. They also could sing after the manner of the Hawaii. The matter of rationing was complicated by the necessity for providing variegated forms of food to suit religion and/or nationality, and the Quartermaster heaved an audible sign of relief on hearing: "Hong Kong, five Officers and sixteen Other Ranks - all omnivorous":

The Officers' Mess showed an equally mixed collection of uniforms; and individuals wandered around obtaining a free lesson in Geography by reading shoulder-titles. Mine were, I regret, somewhat obscure, and I had to explain to more than one curious inquirer that R.H.K.D.F. (pronounced "Rykdof") is an island in the Samoan group mandated to Britain after the First World War. As a West Indian Officer said "One learns things here about the British Empire one never knew before".

We found on arrival a most interesting and comprehensive training programme, comprising graded route-marches, starting at three miles and working upwards; much "gravel bashing" to learn alignment when marching in twelves; and negotiation of obstacles-hurdles being cunningly disposed to represent street-island and such excrescences as Stanhope Gate, Marble Arch and Admiralty Arch. I need scarcely add that our training-programme had to be

The 1953 Coronation Procession in London

scrapped almost at once and we reverted to the time-honoured method of orders for the following day appearing at about 1800 hours. For this no blame could be attached to anyone, least of all to the C.O. Lieut.-Colonel G. N. Ross of the Gordon Highlanders, or the Adjutant, Captain O. W. A Kite of the East Lancashires who did a job which would have tried the patience of a saint, and remained cheerful and efficient throughout; it was due partly to weather and more to the frequent and often unheralded visits of V.V.I.Ps. Omitting lesser lights, on the 25th May we were inspected by the C.I.G.S. General Sir John Harding, who stopped and talked to Francis Quah and C.S.M. Walker. 'You're a P.S.I., of course' said the C.I.G.S. to C.S.M. Walker. Walker's chest swelled about three inches. 'No, Sirr, a Volunteerr with thirrty yearrs serrrvice' he replied. Later in the Mess, the C.I.G.S. disclosed considerable knowledge of operations in the Far East during the late war, and discussed the work of the B.AAG. with Francis Quah. The following morning we were inspected by that very good looking breezy young naval officer, His Royal Highness the Duke of Edinburgh, who descended on us literally "from the skies" as he arrived by helicopter. He was the only one who noticed the rosette on Quah's Pacific ribbon-and knew what it meant. He was suitably impressed by the martial moustache and bearing of Don Luddington, and assumed that both he and Walker were regulars attached to the R.H.K.D.F. as instructors. He told us, which I did not know before, that he had been in "Duke of York" when the fleet relieved Hong Kong in 1945. "Pity you didn't come four yearres soonerr, Sirr" said C.S.M. Walker. The inspection was somewhat marred by what in England they call a heavy rainstorm, and we would call "a spot of damp" - which sent the photographers flying into cover before the Duke reached us.

After drinks with senior officers in the Mess H.R.H. re-entered the helicopter, now surrounded by a ring of Colonial troops, very wet but also very enthusiastic, and ascended heavenwards, while we gazed fervently upward, and the backwash of the rotor sent all headgear flying, and mowed down the front ranks like ripe corn.

Meanwhile we were beginning to get some cohesion among the numerous different contingents, and the formations for the Procession were announced. Since seniority counted from the rear, being nearer to the Queen's coach, the first Group consisted of the Armed Police of eight different parts of the world. These marched twelve abreast, Group 2 comprised the Air Force Auxiliaries of Hong Kong, Singapore and Malaya, with the Aden Arab Levies. This group numbered 42 and so marched in sevens, P/O Peter Donohue of Hong Kong commanded the group and the H.K.A.A.F. formed the front rank. Group 3, in ranks of twelve, comprised two ranks of "Caribees"-the West Indies, Honduras, British Guiana; half a rank (and how we cursed those blank files) of Singapore and Falkland

The 1953 Coronation Procession in London

Islands, then Hong Kong, Malta and Gibraltar, one rank of each. Group 4 comprised Malaya and Fiji, Groups 5 and 6 the various African Contingents, and Group 7 the R.N. and R.N.V.R. Contingents, marching in six (there were only 18 of them). I had a scare on May 24th, the day before our first rehearsal march. Jimmy Lowcock had walked into a gateway and cracked his head open and was hors de combat and likely to remain so! I wasn't unduly concerned about Jimmy's skull, but I cared a lot about our correct numbers as a blank file would look bad. However, he rolled up the following morning with a doctor's certificate saying that he had six stitches in his head and was "fit for active service".

We all thought this a plucky show on his part and the crack on his head seemed to have improved his rifle slope to a marked degree! I may say that the very amicable relations prevailing in the Mess did not extend to the Parade Ground, and one was apt to express oneself with considerable freedom on the shortcomings of members of other contingents who by their faulty footwork had spoilt the otherwise immaculate dressing of one's own rank. Route-marches had been abandoned as the streets around Woolwich are not adapted to troops marching twelve abreast; but we came to know that Parade Ground rather well, as we marched round and round, with and without a band, each rank splitting into two at the Island and into three sections of four at the "Marble Arch". Our first Dress rehearsal took place on May 27th, a colourful scene. The Fijians "stole the picture" with their scarlet blouses, short white "scalloped" skirts and sandals. The Malay Regiment and Malayan Police in white drill with wide coloured sashes ran them close. The African contingents and West Indians mostly affected K.D. shorts and shirts, headgear varying widely and the West Africans adding scarlet monkey-jackets. Malta and Gibraltar preferred S.D.; one or two smaller units wore Battle Dress. As Don Luddington said, we could have turned out in pink silk shorts and Chinese coolie hats and no one would have blinked an eye! Only one other contingent, the British Guianians, wore correct Blues, and they topped it with peculiar black wide-awake hats, which gave them a vaguely clerical aspect, as of swashbuckling Canons. We were at a distinct disadvantage sartorially. The fact was that the members of The Hong Kong Regiment looked too much like regular soldiers just as men of the H.K.A.A.F. looked too much like regular R.A.F. Reporters and photographers assumed that we were portions of the regular army, temporarily involved with the Colonial Contingents, and after a casual glance, departed in search of something more exotic.

After the above dress-rehearsal the Hong Kong Contingent was complimented on their smart appearance and good turn-out in the matter of dress, and my thanks go to the Defence Force tailor who produced our well-fitting tunics.

The 1953 Coronation Procession in London

Meanwhile the lighter side of life was not neglected. The United Empire Association (whom may Allah prosper!) had arranged a most comprehensive list of entertainments, mainly evening, of which the two most popular were Sonia Heinje's Ice Carnival and "The Magic Circle". A fleet of buses each with an Officer in charge transported the contingents. There was always a certain amount of panic lest some unfortunate colonial should be left behind in the trackless jungle of Leicester Square, and before the return journey, worried officers went along the line of buses counting heads and seeking lost sheep, vociferating: "Anyone here seen Somaliland or Trinidad?" - "I say, half of Gibraltar's still missing!" - "Bahamas! I've lost my Bahamas!"- "Where the heck are the Falkland Islands?", etc. Hong Kong, I am glad to say, never erred. It turned up each time intact and correct, wearing a somewhat supercilious air, and usually wiping its lips.

Then on May 28th, in perfect weather, Tony Ford, self, and our respective better halves, and Francis Quah, represented Hong Kong at the Garden Party at Buckingham Palace, where, incidentally, we met Major and Mrs. Bevan Field. Royalty was much in evidence; we were not, however, presented. In that knot of colour culled from all parts of the Empire, only the most exotic stood out. Had we been wearing scarlet pyjamas and purple cummerbunds topped by feathered topees, we might have caught the eye of the gentleman-in-waiting. In our correct No. 1 Blues, we might as well have been in Moss Bros. morning coats. Wonderful indeed were the costumes! Had it really been the Fancy Dress parade it appeared, first prize would have gone to the Sultan of somewhere in Africa, who sported a morning coat with tails reaching the ground, red waistcoat, short knee-length black skirt, long black shins, sandals and yellow gloves. A Nigerian potentate arrived complete with a vast umbrella, borne aloft by a depressed-looking standard-bearer. The umbrella was about the size of a bell-tent, and the said potentate was highly popular with those who were seeking a little shade. I obtained one of his visiting cards, but gave it away later to a souvenir hunting Canadian. For striking appearance there was none to touch Queen Salote of Tonga, 6 foot 4 inches in height, and built somewhat on the generous lines of Miss Tessie O'Shea; and one old friend, Major Takala of Fiji, a vision of white, scarlet and gold, and also wearing the fashionable bare black legs.

And so to Chelsea, where in the magnificent old hall of the Pensioner Hospital, presided over by a portrait of Nell Gwynn, the Minister of State for War and the Chief of the Imperial General Staff received Colonial and Commonwealth officers-and so to Woolwich and bed.

Worthy of mention was the R.A. Mess Night on the 29th, with the Master Gunner, Field Marshal the Viscount Alanbrooke, K.G., G.C.B., O.M., D.S.O.,

The 1953 Coronation Procession in London

(and 25 lesser 'gongs ') - in the chair, and the Hon. Oliver Lyttelton as Guest of Honour - an unforgettable evening. Never again shall I find myself seated betwixt two generals and opposite a Field Marshal. Never again shall I see such a wonderful array of silver tableware and decorations-reputed to be the world's second largest, and the mere cleaning of which is full time employment for two men. Never again shall I witness such interesting and ancient ceremonial ritual; the loyal toast to The Queen-Our Captain General; the ritual passing of the snuff box; the 18th century costumes of the waiters; the lightning-like removal of the table cloths. Yes, a wonderful evening.

Then on May 30th, we entrained and left the fleshpots of Woolwich for the wilderness of Kensington Gardens. Kensington Gardens had been transformed into a camp for some 25,000 troops-a remarkable piece of organisation. And here to greet us was Padre Ogilvie, who found his way to our lines before we did, and who, old soldier that he is, was a great help to us, knowing where and how to procure the amenities of camp life, and producing them as out of a hat. On the 31st, we had a practice march in our formation during the morning and, as a consequence, there was but poor response to the invitation by the Honourable Artillery Company - Hong Kong being represented by Ogilvie, Luddington and self only. The H.A.C. lived up to their reputation for hospitality. Most attractive was the display of pike and arquebus drill, also rear-guard action against cavalry, as laid down in the Military Manual of 1560-when war was a leisurely and dignified amusement, and when a complicated manoeuvre, such as firing a volley, required twenty-three separate and distinct commands.

The Glorious First of June was enhanced for certain of us, Group Commanders and the first ranks of each group, who rose at 0330 hrs, and had a preliminary canter round the 11 1/2 mile course. It was interesting to see the hundreds of street sleepers along the route. Some of these were, of course, Provincials "oop for t'Coronation", but many were Londoners intent on staking out a claim for a place in the front row of spectators. It was a strenuous day for the early risers as they had to turn out with the rest of us at 0900 hrs. for another practice march, but I must say that the H.K.A.A.F., or anyway their seven representatives, can "take it" better than most sergeants. Whoever picked the H.K.A.A.F. representatives did a good job. And so to 'spit and polish' and prognostications regarding the weather.

"And what did you see of the Coronation Procession Daddy?" "The hinder view of the man in front of me, Christopher Robin", I came to know the rearward aspect of that Falkland Islander pretty well as time went on.

Actually, this, the Great Day, started more restfully than any other. Breakfast was leisurely, and it was not until 1043 hrs that Colonial Contingents

The 1953 Coronation Procession in London

moved off, marching by way of Knightsbridge to Birdcage Walk-the Assembly Point. Here we waited and got somewhat wet in the process. Haversack rations were served out, most of which, I think, went to the spectators lining Birdcage Walk. There were four bands. The Durhams, Gloucesters, Royal Scots, and IVth Hussars; two were to play together for ten minutes, after which the other two relieved them. The change of bands was also to be the signal for troops to change arms. The service from the Abbey was broadcast on loudspeakers, but we caught little of it, which was a pity, as it is the most superbly impressive of all services. However, we have all heard it since. During the "actual ceremony, we were called to attention, and there was a complete silence throughout the crowd and the words came through distinctly and clearly.

At 1350 hrs the loudspeaker blared forth. Colonel Burrows took his place at the head of the procession, the bands of the Durhams and Gloucesters struck up, and we moved out into Whitehall, and into a volume of cheering of which I have never heard the like. Wonderful are the English, and especially the Londoners. I can never hope to understand them but my admiration is unstinted. Many of these spectators had been there, not for hours, but for days; others had taken up position the previous night. They had been standing twelve to eighteen hours; they were packed like sardines; they were soaked by rain-and they were enjoying it all immensely. No people on earth can extract pleasure from discomfort like the Londoners can; no people on earth are so orderly-in any other capital city, crowds of that dimension would have been wellnigh uncontrollable. And finally, no people on earth can cheer like the Londoners. You may have heard a crowd at a big football match giving tongue when the deciding goal is scored. That may give a faint perception of the over-powering roar which accompanied us for five and a half miles. The bands, thirty yards in front, were at times almost inaudible. Orders were hopeless. In some cases, Group Commanders gave "change arms" by raising their swords; in other cases, men watched the Group Commanders' mouths.

Now we have left Whitehall and turned left into the Mall and St. James's Street, and then comes Piccadilly, at the end of which there looms our worst obstacle, Stanhope Gate. Here the ranks must split each into three sections to negotiate the three archways, and at the same time we must make a very "tight" right wheel-rather more than 90 degrees. The left files plunge under their archway, stepping out and keeping their fingers metaphorically crossed, and find in emerging that the ranks are in perfect alignment - a very welcome surprise. Now we are in East Carriage Drive, and somewhere on the right is Stand 15 and the Hong Kong spectators. They may be showing encouragement or hiding their heads in shame, but we know not, for no individual sound comes through the roar of noise. Halfway along the Drive we halt - for the procession takes its time from

The 1953 Coronation Procession in London

the rear - the Queen's Coach. A pause, during which the Northern Rhodesians are mistaken by the crowd for Australians and serenaded with "Waltzing Matilda".

A few minutes only, then the signal drops, and we are off again. Marble Arch is ahead, but again we emerge on the other side with ranks perfectly dressed-when marching twelve abreast, a few inches either way makes an enormous difference; and so into Oxford Street, marvellously decorated, could we but spare a glance upward, and here the cheering is even louder.

Into Regent Street with a tricky right wheel necessitating a lot of stepping out on the left, and then easy going along Regent Street and the Haymarket. It is as we pass the corner of Trafalgar Square that the only individual voice is heard - a woman's: "Thanks a lot for coming boys, sorry it was raining". Typical of London. Then Admiralty Arch, an easy one as it was on the straight; and then down the Mall with Colours flying and swords at the carry in one final grand burst. Then Birdcage Walk and the first Dismissal Point.

I think most of us were surprised that it was over so quickly and easily. We still had to march back to Kensington, however, and as there were thousands of spectators even here, there could be no relaxing - until we reached the Gardens. Then into sixes - what a relief. And so back to camp.

There was a certain amount of weariness, not because of the distance, for we were in fine training, but reaction from nervous strain; and the majority decided to call it a day and spend the remaining hours repairing the havoc done by rain and mud. On June 3rd we paraded early, and Commonwealth and Colonial troops marched to Buckingham Palace and formed up on the grass lawns where the Garden Party had been held. At 1100 hrs Her Majesty The Queen inspected us. She looked radiant, and not in the least tired after the previous day's ordeal. She personally decorated the Commandant of the Commonwealth contingents and Colonel Ross. The remainder of the medals were then distributed by Contingent Commanders. Then came the March Past. Her Majesty stood at the top of the steps and took the Salute. This was the first time I had seen the Royal children. Prince Charles, Duke of Cornwall, was on his best behaviour, kept his eye on his father, and saluted in unison with him. Princess Anne conformed for a time with a snappy "ear-tickle", until she caught sight of the Fijians, and deciding that they were really too good to be true gazed spellbound and forgot about such mundane matters as saluting.

It was on this day, incidentally, the sober-clad ones, had something of our own back on the exotically dressed units for it rained heavily, and the rain was followed by a brisk wind from the Arctic regions, against which white or khaki drill, not to mention bare arms and legs, afforded scant protection.

The 1953 Coronation Procession in London

From relatives and friends, who had been in the stands the previous day, we learned details of the procession. The Colonial Contingents, we were informed, had negotiated the Stanhope Gate better than most, and had made a brave show along East Carriage Drive. It appeared that we, at the head of the Procession, took the brunt of the cheering, though other favourites, the "Mounties" in particular, were greeted even more deafeningly. What the cheering was like when Her Majesty went by passes human comprehension. Next in popularity came Sir Winston Churchill, who went by, leaning out of the carriage window, waving his hat and giving the "V" signal with his free hand, and Queen Salote, who, in an open carriage was drenched, and with the water dropping off her appeared to be enjoying herself hugely. Later she told reporters "I do love your English weather". "Linger longer, Queen of Tonga. Let Us really show you!"

June 4th was a busy day. Commonwealth and Colonial Forces broke camp, paraded early, and marched to the Horse Guards where we witnessed the rehearsal of the Trooping the Colour. It was, as might have been expected, a miracle of military precision. Most interesting was the manner in which orders were not shouted, but "sung" and, without apparent effort, the words were clearly audible at a distance of 500 yards. Unfortunately, spectators were rather crowded, and personally I viewed the proceedings hanging by one arm and one leg from the side of a temporary stand - not the best position from which to salute Colours as they come past.

From there to Whitehall, where we formed a hollow square around the Cenotaph, and watched Queen Salote and Sir Arthur Morse laying wreaths; others there were some thirty I believe, representatives of our far-flung Empire; but for obvious reasons these two stood out above the crowd. It was, I fancy, the first public occasion on which Sir Arthur, in this respect, has more than met his match. Thence to the Colonial Office, to be told briefly what fine fellows we were, and to have a closer view of the Queen of Tonga who, for no apparent reason, was among those present. Thence to the Horse Guards again, where haversack rations were served out, and eager sightseers gathered to watch the wild animals feeding and so to London Bridge and home to Woolwich.

June 5th was an "off" day, so the Hong Kong contingent went to Mill Hill to lunch with the Middlesex Regiment (the 2nd Bn, the former 77th), who entertained us right royally. Few old acquaintances were there but Sgt. da Costa greeted us warmly.

On June 6th, we paraded at some unearthly hour and caught a train for Birmingham at 0715 hrs. There, most of the officers were guests of the C.I.G.S. and the Mayor of Birmingham at lunch at the Guildhall. The residue of officers

The 1953 Coronation Procession in London

and the troops did a most interesting tour, which appeared to include most of the noble city from (a) station to restaurant for lunch, (b) restaurant to Drill Hall to don our "glad rags" and (c) Drill Hall to Forming-up Ground. Later we did the same tour in reverse order. In comparison with that, the actual march-about a couple of miles-was nothing. The loudspeakers along the route blared out about the Fiji and Malaya contingents as usual (all in gaudy warpaint) and said divil a word about anyone else, so when the officers went off afterwards to the Guildhall for tea and I was forming up the troops; I gave the order - "JAMAICA - ST. KITTS - TRINIDAD - LEEWARD ISLANDS - WINDWARD ISLANDS - BRITISH HONDURAS - BRITISH GUIANA - MALTA - GIBRALTAR - SINGAPORE - HONG KONG - FALKLAND ISLANDS - A-TEN-SHUN!!" It took a lot of breath but evoked more applause from the spectators than it deserved.

We returned to Woolwich at about 2200 hrs surfeited with food, for in addition to a couple of meals served out on the train and a heavy lunch, the troops, due to a slight error on my part, had to consume two afternoon teas.

That terminated the serious side of things. Much still remains. The Royal Tournament, visits to Madame Tussaud's and such like. The Spithead Review, which will, I fear, have to carry on as best it can with only Tony Ford and Szeto to represent Hong Kong, as the rest of our contingent have to catch the plane back to Hong Kong on that day. We are left with a slight feeling of reaction after what has been our most strenuous time since the last war, and a gradually growing realisation that we have played a part, infinitesimal though it may have been, in the greatest, the most brilliant, and the most impressive Pageant that the world has yet seen.

APPENDIX VIII

Tributes to Colonel E. G. Stewart
O.B.E., D.S.O., E.D.

Tribute by By Brigadier L. T. Ride, C.B.E., E.D.

The last thing that Colonel Evan Stewart would want us to do would be to go to the trouble of writing at length about his life and service as a Volunteer; Evan didn't do things in order to be thanked and he shunned all suggestions of personal publicity and individual demonstrations of every kind; but his main objection would be on the score of the trouble it would be to others. Thoughtfulness and concern for others was one of his very many great qualities and we shall have cause to refer to this again later.

Evan would never shirk a job that needed doing especially if it involved the merest suggestion of duty, or of help to others, or of help to a cause, or if it was of the got-to-be-done type; but when it came to publicity or thanks, he could be more obstinate and difficult than anyone.

This is the sort of conversation that would have taken place had Evan been approached concerning the task that is confronting me now. - "Evan, we want to publish a brief account in the Volunteer about your .army record." - and before I could get any further than that with the proposal, let alone begin to make any request, Evan would interrupt: "Oh Doc" - and that D would be the cause of that fascinating slight stutter which was always accompanied by just the merest twinkle of his eyes and just the slightest suspicion of a smile on his face, all of which were most disarming, and were Evan's successful reaction to attack; they were a most valuable first line of defence, and if and when this was successfully negotiated, one generally found the sting had gone out of the attack altogether. - "Oh Doc", he would continue "you don't want to go to all that trouble." "It's no trouble at all" one would say, not very convincingly, because one was obviously already clearly in trouble with the disarming Evan, "the chaps will want to read something about your record, you know." "Oh that, that's all over and done with and I don't want to be the cause of their wasting their time reading dry and unimportant history, dressed up for display." "But Evan" - the attack is getting very weak by now - "the facts may be unimportant, but what is important is that they should be recorded, for one never knows when a. story like yours may be of help to someone. They are of help in building up pride in the Force, in maintaining morale," etc. etc.; and so it would go on.

Help to others would win the day and as long as it was short and unadorned with embellishments, Evan would agree.

Tributes to Colonel E. G. Stewart, O.B.E., D.S.O., E.D.

I never talked to Evan much about his service during the first world war, but I think his views on that would be that it was hardly worthy of comment; everybody who was worth anything 'went to the war' and that was all there was to it; to talk about trenches and P.H. helmets, duck boards and cloud gas, in military circles in these days would create the same impression as a discourse on punkahs and thunder-boxes would at a cocktail party!

So let us move on to the post World War I period. This was one of the great periods of the Hong Kong Volunteers, it was a period of great recruiting activity and of much development within the Corps, and Evan was in the thick of it all, particularly when there was anything to be done; he let others do most of the arguing, - and there was much of that too, - but that is not to say he had no opinion of his own; he certainly had, but arguing with him had very little effect on them, and arguing about them had no interest for him at all.

No. 3 Company was Evan's great work, his masterpiece, and I shall leave it to Major Field to tell the story of the testing of his creative labours. I shall content myself with merely observing that it is given to few people to build up a fighting machine, to lead it into action and command it throughout its test, and to know in the end that it was not found wanting. That he should be awarded the D.S.O. and be in command of the Hong Kong contingent at the Victory Parade in London after World War II, was a just, though inadequate, recognition of his work for the H.K.V.D.C., the achievements of his Company and of his own bravery in action.

I of course am biased, but in my view Evan's greatest work for the Volunteers still remained to be done; he knew that if he took part in the post-war re-organization he would have to sow for others to reap, but that made no difference to the response of Evan when he knew he was wanted. Military requirements had changed, the volunteer atmosphere was different, yet Evan's reply to the call was the same as it always had been, despite his physical disability. The formation of the Home Guard, development of their wonderful spirit and the success of their achievements, were all due to the work of Evan and a few other stalwarts.

Two events which came at the end of Evan's long service must now be mentioned; they were the award of the O.B.E. and his appointment to be Honorary Colonel of the Hong Kong Regiment; the former was an honour FOR service, the latter an honour WITH service; the former was in recognition of services rendered, the latter gave him the opportunity to continue to perform duties that were still within his power.

Tributes to Colonel E. G. Stewart, O.B.E., D.S.O., E.D.

This was why he placed this appointment above all honours and it was a source of great pleasure to him that he was able to serve on to the last in close association with those who were carrying on the work and the tradition of the organization that he had done so much to build up. Right at the end it worried him not a little that there was nothing more he could do, but the end revealed the true Evan and he remained the Evan we knew of old, right to the last.

A few days before he died I had the pleasure of visiting the Home Guard in camp and I promised them that I would give their former Commanding Officer their best wishes. By this time Evan could neither speak nor make any signs, but mentally he was still very active and as I mentioned each name, his face would light up with what was left of that smile we all knew so well; I feel sure as he lay in hospital with his thoughts, he had many a mental march-past of the No. 3 Company, the H.K.V.D.C., the Home Guard and the Hong Kong Regiment.

His wishes concerning his funeral were typical of him and when it was known what these were, they were respected, and the suggestion was not pressed that there should be a military funeral; there were many reasons which contributed to this decision, but not the least was his dislike of personal publicity and his determination not to he the cause of any additional burden to the heavy duties of others. His funeral was therefore a private one and it was at the Memorial Service held at St. John's Cathedral on 23rd December 1958 that so many of his former comrades, and his numerous friends in other walks of life, were able to pay their last respects to their revered comrade-in-arms, together and without distinction or differentiation.

Tributes to Colonel E. G. Stewart, O.B.E., D.S.O., E.D.

Tribute by By Major B. C. Field, M.B.E., M.C., E.D.

Although I had been acquainted with Colonel Stewart for several years, I first got to know him well when I was posted to No. 3 Company H.K.V.D.C. in 1940. Colonel Stewart then had under his command about 100 Volunteers in four Platoons.

We spent most of our time in that last year before the War digging machine gun emplacements and trenches on the hillsides above such places as Magazine Gap, Wanchai Gap and Middle Gap. Being spread out rather for one Company, each Platoon had to work pretty much on its own, but I will always remember, behind it all, the kindly but keen eye and ubiquitous presence of our O.C. He never seemed to be still and we could always count on him turning up when we were out in the hills.

He seemed to know all that was going on and who was doing what, without having to be told. That was his genius, to know people, and it was reassuring to us to feel that he did know, because he was there to help, not to find fault. He was kind and understanding. He never had to take any nonsense from anyone because we all respected him and liked him so much that we did our best not to let him down in any way.

We were a very happy crowd in No. 3 Company. There was a sort of cheerful eagerness combined with loyalty which made it easy to get things done. No nagging or shouting or quarrelling. That was, I am sure, because the Company had a leader who was strong enough to put us all more or less unconsciously on our best behaviour.

As things turned out in the Battle of Hong Kong that spirit proved to be just about the most valuable thing we had, as a, fighting unit. I often used to wonder what it was that made so many of those Volunteers respond so well in the face of what they all knew to be a pretty bad situation.

Thinking about it now, after all these years, I am more than ever convinced that it was Even Stewart's leadership and example during those months of training before the show started that in a queer sort of way made us all, in varying degrees, counterparts of our O.C. Without having to think about it, or even know what it was so, we had something of Evan's gallant heart inside each one of us.

What a happy, delightful man he was! If he was ever afraid of anything I never once saw him show it. I remember one day on Stonecutters, most of us had never been under fire before and, I must confess, it does take some getting used to. They had three guns somewhere over near Kam Tin and an O.P. on Needle

Hill, so we were told, and every now and then the shells would come over three at a time, like steam engines, and crash into the island.

Once when the shelling in the West Battery area was particularly bad I was on my way back to Company Headquarters near South Pier. As I got nearer to where the shells were coming down I kept one eye an the next handy bit of cover all the time, ready to dive for it at a moment's notice, and felling very far from happy. Then I heard voices coming along the path, and there was Evan with a couple of Volunteers, strolling along as if the war was a thousand miles away. I was glad to see him and much comforted. We stood and chatted for a few moments and in that time three more shells came over. I'm afraid I crouched down instinctively, but Evan just stood there, as if he was visiting my Platoon area at Middle Gap on a training afternoon before the balloon went up. When I straightened up again, feeling rather ashamed of myself, he just went on talking as if nothing had happened. I had a warm feeling of deep gratitude and respect, respect for his coolness and gratitude for not noticing. After that I felt better about the shelling and soon realised with a happy sort of relief that I was not going to be so scared after all. Evan had somehow in his kindly magic way given me sufficient of his own courage and trust to carry me through the days that were to follow.

When the No. 3 Company Headquarters area was attacked just before dawn, on the 19th December, 1941, Evan was in the Headquarters battle shelter just west and below the A.A. emplacement. He took a rifle and went up the stepped path to see what was going on. The A.A. people in the emplacement there were taking heavy punishment from small arms and mortar fire, and within a few moments Evan had been shot through the right shoulder. He promptly brought up his rifle and returned the fire, but the shock of the recoil on his damaged shoulder was enough for even such a man and they got him back to the battle shelter where they patched him up a little. He stayed in that shelter with six others for three days. Enemy soldiers were all round but did not go down to the shelter, possibly because it was on the exposed side of the hill

They never thought of coming out and surrendering. What they hoped for was a counterattack and they were ready to join in. But at last they had to accept the fact that the counterattack was not coming, and on the third night they left in pairs, at fifteen minute intervals, quietly slid over the wall in front of the shelter and down the steep hillside to Happy Valley. Evan, typically, was the last to leave, and he was lucky to get away because by that time the sentries were suspicious and opened fire at the slight noise he made getting over the wall. Fortunately it was a pitch black night and he was not hit.

Tributes to Colonel E. G. Stewart, O.B.E., D.S.O., E.D.

Evan got his shoulder cleaned up at the Hong Kong Hotel dressing station and then with his arm in a sling went straight off to find the remnants of No. 3 Company, hardly a platoon strong, now holding part of the line in the Wanchai area. By that time he had been almost constantly awake and for much of the time under fire or in close contact with the enemy for thirteen days. Wounded and in considerable discomfort, yet he was still not satisfied with a purely defensive role. Lt. Col. E. J. R. Mitchell told me after the war that Evan had phoned him at Volunteer Headquarters, then on the Peak, reporting strength and asking to be put back into the battle!

And so he remained, the same fearless irrepressible Evan, all through those tiresome, though occasionally alarming, years that followed. Once in Shamshiupo Camp, during an air raid, an ebullient young airmen dived on the camp with a clattering screaming roar of engine and cannon fire, and shot up the length of the wide road which ran through the camp. We all dived under our beds - an automatic though futile reaction - all except Evan, who apparently noticed nothing, but just sat on his bed and got on with some reading he was doing at the time.

He was different from the rest of us. Usually when a man is different people dislike him, but with Evan that was not so because I think we knew that he had a sort of strength which we could share, someone with us who was not afraid.

There are times when we all need someone like that and it is for that more than anything that I will remember him.

Now Evan has gone where so many of his men of No. 3 Company were waiting to greet him. Those of us who remain are better and happier for having known him. One by one we shall no doubt rejoin the ranks, and Evan will be there, in his easy happy way, gallantly leading us on into that receding, ever widening tapestry which records the story of Volunteering in Hong Kong.

Index

Index of those named in the Record of the Actions of the Hong Kong Volunteer Defence Corps in the Battle for Hong Kong, December 1941 including an index to the units with the indexing of the Hong Kong Volunteer Defence Corps down to platoon level.

The following abbreviations are used for those who were not members of the HKVDC, the Hong Kong Volunteer Defence Corps

BAAG	Bristh Army Aid Group based in China
HKRNVR	Hong Kong Royal Naval Volunteer Reserve
HKSRA	Hong Kong and Singapore Royal Artillery
KSLI	King's Scottish Light Infantry
IF	Innis Fusiliers
MX	Middlesex
PJ	Punjab Rifles
RA	Royal Artillery
RAFVR	Royal Air Force Volunteer Reserve
RAMC	Royal Army Medical Corps
RAOC	Royal Army Ordnance Corps
RASC	Royal Army Supply Corps
RCAMC	Royal Canadian Army Medical Corps
RM	Royal Marines
RN	Royal Navy
RNVR	Royal Naval Volunteer Reserve
RP	Rajput Rifles
RRoC	Royal Rifles of Canada
RS	Royal Scots
WG	Winnipeg Grenadiers

Index

Index

Index

Index

Index

Index